decline
and
renewal

decline and renewal

Causes and Cures of Decay
among Foreign-Trained Intellectuals
and Professionals in the Third World

CRAUFURD D. GOODWIN, Duke University
MICHAEL NACHT, University of Maryland

The Institute gratefully acknowledges special grant support
from the Exxon Education Foundation and the
United States Agency for International Development
that made publication of this book possible.

INSTITUTE OF INTERNATIONAL EDUCATION
809 UNITED NATIONS PLAZA, NEW YORK, N.Y. 10017

Table of Contents

A Time
to Rethink
International Educational
Exchange

Reflection on our travels and conversations has led us to conclude that now is the time for all parties to rethink the implications of international scholarly and professional exchange. As we review the remarkable flows of intellectuals across borders and between cultures over the past several decades, we marvel at the accomplishments. However, at the same time, we believe that the rationale for these flows has, in general, been too limited; in consequence, the mechanism to facilitate the movement of people remains still not fully developed.

The rationale presented to date has roughly three parts. First, scholars from one country, both junior and senior, should study in another country to gain breadth of comprehension, perspective on their own condition, and appreciation for others. Second, the rich nations have an obligation to open their doors to students from less fortunate nations, with the expectation that these students will return home after graduation to put their newfound skills to good use in the development process. Third, international exchange fosters certain forms of research and scholarly inquiry that cannot be conducted as well, or at all, in one nation alone. In the case of cooperation among scholars from the First and Third Worlds, fields that often require access to more than one country include archeology, plant and animal research, and epidemiology. Programs of international educational exchange have been predicated substantially on these three justifications.

We suggest that there is an important fourth justification. In order for the intellectual and professional sectors of many nations to thrive in the years to come, they must develop close, constructive links with their counterparts in the global community. Moreover, these links must be cumulative and continuing and must produce interactions that are beneficial to all parties. How these links are to be forged remains an open question, but the challenge of their design is an exciting one. On a steadily contracting planet, with inexorably increasing economic integration and threats to human survival, the health of the intellectual community of any nation is of central concern to all others. John Donne's observation that "no man is an island" was never more true.

A vigorous response to the opportunity to assist Third World countries resist professional and intellectual decay can be defended in the First World on grounds of self-interest: on the rising tide of a healthy world economy all boats float upward. But there are moral reasons as well. Those who may be protected from decay through international cooperation often come from humble origins and have few resources on which to fall back. Moreover, these are the persons who must be counted on to build just, as well as efficient, societies in these new nations.

We hope that this report will draw more attention to the problems and opportunities presented by the potential for resistance against intellectual and professional decay in the Third World and that leaders of both worlds will work together to discover and implement cures. It was sometimes remarked to us that the questions we raised related to problems somewhere over the horizon: the immediate challenge to new nations, we were told, is to survive the crisis of the moment. We recognize this difference in perspective but suggest that insistence on a long-term view is a legitimate position for one party in the North-South partnership to take, especially since we feel confident that it will be to everyone's benefit. We like the metaphor suggested to us by one Turkish intellectual. He said that the early days of international educational exchange, when a single training period was considered sufficient, were a "honeymoon." It all seemed so easy and so much fun. Now the challenge is to work out stable long-term relationships in a lasting marriage.

I.
Introduction

During the summer of 1982, we undertook the first project in a new program of research for the Institute of International Education. In the report *Absence of Decision* (IIE, 1982), we described the policies, or lack thereof, in American institutions of higher education toward the rapidly increasing flows of students from other countries that were crowding through their doors. We also suggested issues that should be addressed by American colleges and universities constructing policies toward their international students.

One of the important considerations in the formation of American institutional policy, which remained largely unexplored in 1982, is the effect of American higher education on students from abroad. In order to cast light on this issue, we visited Brazil during the summer of 1982 to prepare a case study and reported our findings in *Fondness and Frustration* (IIE, 1983). The essence of our findings is expressed in the title. The Brazilian alumni were remarkably appreciative of their U.S. experience and conscious of its value, but at the same time they were frustrated by aspects of their subsequent professional life in Brazil. In particular they complained about the rapidity with which they lost the skills and competencies that they had acquired, usually at great cost and sacrifice, during their residence in the United States. We were able to record these concerns in our report and to speculate about them in a general way.

In view of the widespread expressions of concern about intellectual and professional decay, it seemed to many with whom we talked, and increasingly to us as well, that the problem of building up human capital in developing countries involved much more than an initial infusion of training during a brief one-time educational period abroad. It required continuing attention, which some of our correspondents appropriately termed 'aftercare.' In our view it behooved the countries of the Third World, and those in the First World that could offer help, to explore more thoroughly and to understand better the development of human capital.

In this third report, we offer the findings of a more extensive study conducted in Mexico, Indonesia, and Turkey during 1984 and 1985 to provide better understanding of the problem of intellectual and professional decay, to assess its seriousness, and to propose solutions.

We are exceptionally grateful to innumerable new friends for assisting us through terra incognita, especially Norman Goodman and Rene Greenwald,

1

IIE representatives in Indonesia and Mexico respectively. In Turkey we enjoyed the astute guidance and delightful colleagueship of Dr. Zehra Avsar Keye of the University of Minnesota, without whose collaboration our accomplishments would have been markedly inferior. Mr. Arturo Borja provided valuable assistance with our exploration of the Mexican cases. As during our earlier visit to Brazil, we found most of the hundreds of persons with whom we talked cordial, cooperative, and deeply concerned about the subject of our inquiry. We are enormously appreciative of their hospitality and hope that these pages will be useful to them. Finally, we are most grateful to Elinor Barber of the Institute of International Education and David Court of the Rockefeller Foundation for making valuable comments on a draft of this report.

The goal of this study, like those of its two predecessors, is to enrich understanding of developments that are of immense and growing significance to both the First and Third Worlds. We hope at least to provide modest enlightenment, to raise consciousness of issues hitherto inadequately attended to in both worlds, to inspire future research, and to point the way to new policies and programs of interest to prospective grantors and grantees in international education. We hope that we have produced a stimulating, provocative report that may not posit new doctrine but that will pose relevant questions and alternative answers. We think that we can discern, and we do indeed suggest, the outlines of appropriate policy at both ends of international exchange. However, in most areas, the state of our understanding is still too primitive to allow confident, precise prescriptions for action.

This project was made possible with grants from the Exxon Education Foundation and the U.S. Agency for International Development.

II.
Dimensions of the Problem and Our Approach to It

Definitions and metaphors. Intellectual and professional decay is not a notion that we invented in the United States for application to the Third World. Instead it is a concept that was forced upon us repeatedly in conversations with foreign alumni of American universities. We do not suggest that the problem is peculiar to developing countries or to any special group of human beings. It is experienced as a fact of life by all skilled persons, young and old, from the north and south, east and west. In this country it is as serious a threat at the most prestigious research universities and national laboratories as it is at community colleges and high schools. However, there are various peculiar, even unique, characteristics of intellectual and professional decay that are manifested internationally, and there is utility in examining decay as an international phenomenon.

There are several ways to conceive of the phenomenon. Economists may think of it as disinvestment or "human decapitalization," while educators may speak of the obsolescence of teaching capacities or the decline of competence. Political scientists and sociologists may perceive "decayed" intellectuals and professionals as dissatisfied, disappointed, discouraged components of national elites who become destabilizing, destructive forces in their societies. Nations in which decay takes place regret the loss of a national resource. Donors of foreign assistance, who make possible advanced training, are concerned with the eventual decrease in effectiveness of this training. The phenomenon, then, is multifaceted and widely relevant; this section is an attempt to visualize and cast light upon it.

We find an elaboration of the biological metaphor of decay in an organic substance to illuminate the matters that we are addressing. There appear to be two dimensions to the process of intellectual decay, just as there are two in nature. First, there is inevitable aging: humans acquire knowledge and skills and, sooner or later, both humans and their knowledge and skills grow old and fall prey to the weaknesses to which all flesh is heir. Second, there is the pathological element in the process of decay. Like a disease, decay, if unconstrained, causes degeneration in the host more rapidly than it would naturally occur: in the normal aging process, the manifestations of pathological decay are analogous to the symptoms of a disease that may be controlled or even reversed through appropriate medical intervention. The medical profession can ease and delay to some degree the normal course of human aging. It may, through therapy, eliminate pathological aging. In the same way agents of society should be able both to retard, or ease, the part of intellectual decay that is "normal" and to arrest the part that is truly pathological.

To pursue the medical analogy one step further, we can view the recommendations for public and private action at the conclusion of this report as having two dimensions. In one respect they are suggestions for geriatric policy to make the most efficient and humane use of an aging population. But in another respect they suggest therapies to resist, retard, or even cure a disease that strikes with varying degrees of virulence and that, in the views of some, may reach epidemic proportions. Moreover, there are roles both for curative medicine, to deal with the damage that has already been done by the disease, and for preventive medicine by specialists in public health, to prescribe the conditions under which the disease is most likely not to occur.

Another respect in which the medical analogy is useful is in the justification of our rather elaborate attempt to describe and clarify intellectual decay. Even though we do not yet satisfactorily understand its causes, as we do not understand those of many diseases, we know the problems it creates both because those who suffer from decay complain of them and because their effects on society are widely perceived as deleterious. Intellectual decay appears to be a multidimensional syndrome with multiple causes. Additionally, both its manifestations and its origins are unusually difficult to measure. Especially in the countries of the Third World, longitudinal data on indicators of decay are largely nonexistent.

Why this study now? We are persuaded that, despite the difficulties with description and explanation, intellectual and professional decay is far too serious a problem to be ignored or put aside until more confident analysis of it is at hand. Foreign training is certain to remain a requirement for developing countries during the foreseeable future, and problems of professional maintenance are bound to increase steadily. Consequently, in this report our style is more akin to that of the medical clinician who often must treat a disease before it is satisfactorily understood, simply because it is there and people hurt, rather than to that of the medical scientist who must not settle for less than a scientifically defensible explanation.

4

We shall attempt to describe the decay syndrome as fully and richly as we can from the testimony of the sufferers and from our observations of them. Then we shall set forth, in general terms, therapies that, from our explorations, show promise of successful results. Finally, we shall describe a series of case studies of actual attempts in the First and Third Worlds to treat the problem, or potentially do so, both for what illumination these cases may shed on the phenomenon in general and for what guidance they may provide to persons anywhere in the world who face the demanding challenge of formulating responsive policy and action.

It can be argued that intellectual and professional decay is so pervasive in humankind that it should be explored in a wider context than simply that of the developing nations of the Third World and even there among primarily a subset of persons trained abroad. To this we respond that the problem of understanding this phenomenon is sufficiently large that progress on it may better be made through small bites than full mouthfuls. Furthermore, this exploration is undertaken designedly for an audience of readers in both the First and Third Worlds who have a special interest in the welfare and continued effectiveness of this special group of returned international students. Moreover, because in the Third World higher education must be perceived, as economists would say, as mainly a producer good rather than a consumer good (as it is in much of the First World), the decline in its productivity must be seen as a serious social concern, especially when rates of return on competing physical capital goods are particularly high. To the extent that this report does in fact cast light on the larger question of intellectual and professional decay throughout humankind, this is a by-product of the primary intent.

The larger considerations involved. The three countries that we visited had several characteristics in common with one another, as well as with other nations in the Third World. First, at the time they were all to some degree turning **inward**, focusing on questions of identity and nationhood. What should be their relationship to the West? To the East? On what should they model their economies, societies, and policies? Should Karl Marx, John Locke, or Ayatollah Khomeni be seen as the appropriate Messiah? What should be the roles of indigenous culture, values, and religion in national life? What losses of identity were suffered from close relationships with other nations? How should they arrange for the constructive interaction and development of the main institutions in their societies (of which those inhabited by our interviewees were among the most prominent, including universities, public bureaucracies, large corporations, and the media)? We sensed a growing realization that these questions could not be answered easily but found evidence that they were being faced openly and constructively in a way that had not occurred widely since World War II.

Decolonization brought with it not only a rush for independence but frequently also a naive faith in the ease of institutional imitation and adaptation and in the ability to gain true cultural independence. "Development" can be accomplished, according to this way of thinking, simply by copying those farther up the ladder of growth. Foreign-trained intellectuals and professionals should take an essential part in this growth process by learning about those models abroad, bringing them home, and then playing leading roles in their local adaptation. When it is found that these professionals and intellectuals, like the institutions they lead, do not perform precisely as expected and, more importantly, do not seem able to deliver exactly the developmental achievements that had been anticipated, disillusionment and even anger set in. When national crises of an economic, political, social, international, or religious kind intervene, rage and retribution against universities, the professions, a free press, the senior bureaucracy, and other homes for highly trained persons are likely to be the result. Incidents of this kind have, at different times in recent years, characterized all the countries we visited.

Clearly these actions are partly a search for a scapegoat. Disappointment can be assuaged by throwing a body from the castle, and the foreign-trained intellectual is often the most conspicuous body at hand. In part these actions are also based simply on mindless prejudice against elites, which has characterized almost every period of political and social turmoil. But, in some part at least, the resentment of foreign-trained persons, and the seeming delight in — rather than regret of — their decay, grow out of a reasoned sense of the drag these persons impose on a distinctive national development. As carriers of well-formed values and traditions from an alien culture, the foreign-educated constrain the authenticity and spontaneity of development and limit the options for review for a new nation with a whole history ahead of it. In addition, at times these elites are viewed as the successors to their colonial predecessors, equally insensitive to the traditions of their mother nation.

When viewed in this way, some of what we treat as loss of intellectual and professional competence becomes instead reacculturation and reduced dependence on models and habits of thought acquired slavishly in youth. We appreciate this complexity in education and socialization and urge the reader to do so as well. At the same time, the experience of the American melting pot and of other older new nations should be remembered. These nations grew up dependent on a varied infusion of intellectual traditions that taught, above all, the possibility of choice and the importance of tolerance. The testimony of the alumni of American universities whom we interviewed in Brazil persuaded us that the experience they derived was above all a liberating, not a constraining, one. We ourselves remain convinced that rigorous foreign training will continue to be of enormous value to any new and developing society for many years, even if the nation must be mindful always to keep foreign training the servant, never the master, of national destiny.

A second, and superficially contradictory, tendency that was also visible in each of the three countries we visited was to turn **outward** as well as inward. The most important manifestation of such cosmopolitanism (called by one Turk an "extrovert phase") is to place increased emphasis on export growth and extension of international trade rather than on domestic protection and import substitution along the road to development. The significance for our subject of this opening to the world is considerable. If competition is now to be global instead of local there is simply no alternative to pursuing it with the best people and the best training. Whether the export good is tomatoes or electronic components, there is no option other than to produce it with the most efficient and modern techniques. The result of an alternative strategy would be inevitable economic loss and possible bankruptcy.

The strategy of international competition implies training at the best centers, wherever they may be. The same implication holds for the development of social, political, and economic infrastructures. A nation simply cannot sustain a successful export economy without appropriate taxes, a stable money supply, efficient communication, and satisfactory labor relations. Anything less than production under contextual conditions as agreeable as those of one's competitors prevents successful participation in the world economy as surely as use of an obsolete technology does.

The role of foreign-trained specialists during a nation's opening to the world is multifaceted. These people are accustomed to competing on a global stage and may be prepared to show to others how this is done. They also either have knowledge of the international frontier at hand or are equipped to locate it.

The care and feeding of people with the best international training becomes especially critical during an opening to the world. Their loss of a competitive edge in this circumstance may also mean a loss of competitiveness for the nation. Their operations in world markets make them more internationally mobile. They are more likely to migrate if not remunerated, supported adequately, and assisted in maintaining their special competencies and qualities.

In this report we are certainly not attempting to prescribe precisely what national policies should be pursued toward persons who have advanced overseas training in light of national turns inward and outward. The policies must take into account aggregate social objectives, values, and overall development strategies. Our own preferences may indeed show through, but these are not important. We do assert confidently, however, that the question of how to attend to these people is of crucial importance for developing nations and that nations ignore it at their peril.

Our method. We did not administer a set questionnaire to those persons with whom we talked on our three country visits because our primary goal was to describe a phenomenon that most of our respondents did not immediately recognize, were sometimes defensive about, and, like us, did not fully understand. We interviewed academics, students, government officials, journalists, businesspeople, unattached intellectuals, and others who seemed likely to have interesting reflections on our subject. Probing, free-flowing conversation seemed the best route to illumination, and in fact it was. We did not attempt to arrange interviews according to a randomized process, and we did not set up a control group in order to contrast those who were foreign-trained with those who were educated at home. We did this for several reasons.

First, anyone who has attempted to conduct interviews with senior members of the elites of Third World countries knows the problems of operating according to a tight plan: the interviewer cannot randomly pick out for interview from a list Director General X rather than Director General Y; X may be unwilling to see you or traveling abroad, while Y suddenly has a half hour free. Second, it is never clear who is likely to be the most helpful, thoughtful, and communicative interviewee until the discussion begins. For our purpose serendipity often seemed the best route to understanding. For example, X observes, "Now that I think about it, Y has thought hard on that subject." After you have found Y, he tells you that Z has done a relevant study: "You must go and see if he will help you." So much for any plans to interview randomly. Third, it must be emphasized that our objective was not to assess the relative significance for intellectual and professional decay of such different characteristics within our universe as domestic training versus foreign training or German training versus American training so much as to understand the problem as it is. Our focus was on those who received their training abroad for the purpose of discovering what could be done to ameliorate the conditions that affect them.

During the first part of this report we identify by country relatively few of the illustrations that we use to make our points. This is because we did not want to seem to be casting aspersions where none are intended and also because in most cases we found comparable examples in all the countries we visited.

We were pleased to discover that both *Absence of Decision* and *Fondness and Frustration* have stimulated conventional social science research in the areas we explored in these preliminary works. We hope this study will have the same result.

III.
Manifestations and Characteristics of Intellectual and Professional Decay

Indicators of trouble. The most tangible, obvious features of intellectual and professional decay are declines in the effectiveness of "decayed persons" in performing the functions for which they were trained (for example, teaching, research, and the exercise of professional skills). If the progress of the decay is visualized, it may over time take the shape of a characteristic S-shaped curve, with an initial period of low decay (typically three to five years) followed by intense decay and then diminution, since little content in which decay can occur remains.

Sometimes the declines in output are manifested directly in quantitative measures, such as in a drop in the number of scientific papers written, graduate students sponsored, or professional services delivered. But much more often the declines are represented by less tangible, but potentially far more important, qualitative changes. Research is no longer at the cutting edge of a discipline; it no longer takes account of international experience and accumulated knowledge nor responds to the priorities of the scholarly and scientific community and the applied needs of society. Professional practice makes use of tools and devices long since rejected or superseded in that profession. Teaching becomes anachronistic and obsolete and sometimes even comes to represent, over the lifetime of the teacher, the conditions in that discipline of the time when the teacher received graduate training.

We heard numerous assertions of the seriousness of such declines. One psychologist told us of a colleague who still used, in his classes, photocopies of the long-discredited textbooks he had purchased during his graduate education abroad in the 1940s. We were also told of a professor in another field who prohibited his students from citing works published after the date, many years before, when he had received his own Ph.D. In these and comparable extreme cases, the productivity of the foreign-trained persons had actually become negative. Their students were being taught what was no longer the accepted truth.

The notion of declining productivity among those who experience professional and intellectual decay implies some judgment about the value of the goods and services produced by the persons. Two qualifications of this judgment must be stressed. First, the training received abroad by some students may be inappropriate both for their own careers and for their nations' needs. In such cases, decay of inappropriate skills does not represent a real decline in productivity but rather represents rapid depreciation, or write-off, of human capital constructed in error in the first place. This form of decay frequently occurs because many students from developing countries who study in the United States are exposed to concepts, techniques, and subject areas that have limited or no applicability in their own societies. Second, some apparent decay and decline in productivity may simply represent career readjustments for which people's advanced training indirectly equipped them and that serve both national and personal interests. Well-known examples of these career redirections are scholars who leave their disciplines to become administrators or "institution builders," and scientists and professionals in the public service who abandon specializations to become generalist senior bureaucrats. The extent of such exceptions seems to vary over time and will be discussed with the causes of decay.

Manifestations of decay that are less clearly identifiable than changes in outputs and that are in many cases a prelude to declines in visible productivity are also important. Interviewees emphasized to us what they referred to as loss of touch with a discipline or profession. "It is partly that you don't know what is on people's minds in your area," one Mexican scientist told us, "but it is also that you no longer know where to find out." An Indonesian scientist wistfully remarked to us, "You can't stay in the game unless you're on the field." The sense of being "out of it," especially after having recently come from a vigorous community of scholars in a graduate program of a major research university abroad, seems to be exceptionally dispiriting and to lead to regrettable consequences. "Apart from whether or not you can still conduct teaching and research on the frontier of your subject," one Mexican academic told us, "if you don't have close touch any more you lose the will to try."

A wide variety of adjectives were used to describe the condition of decay. A Turkish psychologist said that after 15 years away from centers of research in the United States she felt "demoted and stale." She needed most of all "professional exchange of ideas" and "peer intervention." Despite a seeming amplitude of vigor, she described herself as needing external motivation and competition, someone to "wind her spring." Another psychologist, more recently returned, described herself as "disoriented and depressed, angry, discouraged, and helpless." A prominent business leader, trained at a major business school, added that without the stimulus of international competition, "you lose your edge and your balance to the point that you don't realize you have fallen behind."

A complex aspect of decay that was explained to us by a group of scientists in Turkey was the difficulty encountered in maintaining a position on the scientific frontier when the frontier moved so quickly that it could not be seen by their employers and funding agencies. They explained, for example, that cell and molecular biology were still viewed with some suspicion, while biotechnology was seen as a fad that could safely be ignored. They suggested that some programs of First World nations, especially in the sciences, should be aimed at rendering new research dimensions visible and credible to countries of the Third World.

Loss of morale. The large issue of loss of morale also figured prominently in the less tangible manifestations of decay that scholars and scientists drew to our attention. They related it to what one called the "ethic of research." A frequent refrain we encountered was that graduate or professional training in the West results in changes in style and attitude as much as in knowledge of subject matter. A student learns such things as professionalism, assertiveness, openness to innovation ("change orientation"), discipline in approaching problems, timeliness, scientific standards, hard work, self-confidence in playing on a world stage, and the excitement of discovery. One very impressive Turkish engineer, now the head of a large consulting firm, emphasized above all the tradition he had picked up in America of commitment to rapid completion of tasks, which had led to a high degree of synergism among professionals in his own company. "The harder we work, the more efficient we become."

These qualities of style and behavior are all exceptionally fragile and may deteriorate as rapidly as scientific skills or effective participation in a professional community. This fact is significant because loss of these qualities is often a prelude to the ultimate decay of intellectual vigor and scientific accomplishment. An important element in the "ethic of research," which, as we were told, is insufficiently appreciated in the Third World, is that continued research and inquiry on the frontier of a discipline are valuable not only for the new knowledge they yield but also for the constant refreshment they afford to the practical skills of the researcher.

It appeared to us and to our interviewees that the prevalence and seriousness of decay vary among different segments of the intellectual and professional communities. Decay seems to be most severe in "mixed" professions in which individuals try to combine two or more careers (for example, research scholar, teacher, practitioner, and administrator). Full-time specialists in any one field seem to fare best over time. Not surprisingly, perhaps, proximity to, or presence in, a metropolis is another significant variable. In all three countries, people in the provinces seem to experience decay sooner, with fewer opportunities to redress their decline. Similarly, people in certain occupations and specialties complain of decay more readily. Employees throughout the general public service seem especially vulnerable to decay, while, in contrast, central bank economists seem relatively immune. Among particular disciplines it seems that those with a clear specialization resist decay better than those with a generalist orientation. A Turkish civil engineer claimed that a high proportion of what he had learned in an advanced-degree program in the United States remained highly relevant to his work, but all of the local rules and regulations, as well as informal customs and practices, placed pressure on him to forget everything he had learned abroad and to revert to old ways. He felt that some sort of steady refreshment was crucial to sustain his convictions and self-confidence.

Several people described to us what they knew to be a downward spiral into decay. An initial manifestation of decay in teaching or research leads quickly to a lack of credibility either at home or in the international community. This, in turn, cuts off access to funding, travel, and the means to recover from the initial slip. The downward spiral continues with further loss of morale, missed deadlines, lost credibility, and eventual departure from the field or discipline. The rector of one prominent Mexican university reported that in certain fields the average duration of appointment had fallen to three years, reflecting the abandonment of academic careers by young persons who had completely lost faith in their prospects. It was widely agreed that once the downward spiral has begun it is extremely difficult to bring about a reversal.

Differential rates of recognition. It seems to us that among those with whom we talked members of the private business sector and the professions (for example, law, medicine, and accounting) best understand the decay problem. They belive that it threatens their profitability and, in some cases, even their survival. (In some professions, such as journalism, the nature of the occupation seems to minimize this hazard.) People in academic institutions are the next most realistic. In varying degrees they appreciated the problems and have programs underway to cope with them. (We did meet with a few recalcitrant university administrators who deny that it is anyone's responsibility other than the individual faculty member's to stay abreast of the latest developments in the field.) Persons involved in the public service seem least aware and least concerned, telling us often that loss of intellectual and professional competence is a nonproblem.

It was remarked to us that persons who had had high school or undergraduate education in the United States are faced with a peculiar kind of decay. In a sense their reentry problems never come to an end. Cultural dilemmas, which in many cases overwhelm their intellectual and professional lives, are created. Persons with only a master's degree gained abroad, it was said, often do not know how to recognize decay. Persons with high-powered Ph.D.'s, on the other hand, are sometimes inclined to exaggerate the problem. Typically they are already culturally formed by the time of their study abroad and their problems later come mainly in maintaining their disciplinary skills. The mere loss of the intimacy with the research frontier that they had built up during graduate school seems to them to be evidence of terminal decline.

As a subject of serious research, or even focused concern, we discerned only the beginnings of attention to the problem of intellectual decay in the countries we visited. We hope that this condition will be reversed in the years ahead.

Stages of decay. Some thoughtful observers of national development in their countries suggested that there is a three-stage sequence in the evolution of their advanced manpower needs. First, they need managers, organizers, facilitators, and communicators. Next, they require builders, teachers, and developers who will extend the modern sector and involve an increasing portion of the population in the life of the nation at a relatively rudimentary level. Decay of skills and competencies is certainly a problem in these early stages, but in the third stage it becomes acute. The need then is to develop large cadres of skilled personnel in government, the private sector, and academe with competencies equal to the best anywhere in the world.

After a certain point, growth requires competition on an open world stage where the penalty for poor performance is national failure. The challenges to conduct and apply innovative research and to develop the sophisticated training and professional skills required for a complex and highly integrated world economy and society necessitate both large numbers of competent persons and the highest standards. In this third stage the costs of decay become truly intolerable and insupportable. At the time we visited Indonesia, the country had recently announced plans to acquire 18,000 engineers with advanced skills, mainly through overseas training of their young people. It was clear that the problem of maintaining the skills of this large cadre would reach this country on a scale never dreamed of before. We were told that in the 1960s Turkey had seen a vigorous development of training in business administration. Twenty years later, the problem of obsolescence and maintenance of competence in that field was becoming intense for the first time.

We were struck by the analogy of a person who at a certain stage of rapid growth in wealth acquires an expensive automobile or other consumer durable. This person knows well the capital cost but may not know, or be willing to provide for, the costs of the maintenance and depreciation of this durable. Failure to do so, of course, leads to collapse of the equipment and potentially to disillusionment with the entire investment process.

Another stage theory frequently described to us concerns the participation of foreign assistance agencies in the development process. These agencies, their critics said, are hostage to a mistaken theory of discontinuous growth that conveniently justifies their own precipitous departure from the scene when, supposedly, a nation or a sector reaches the stage of self-sustaining growth. The result of this theory and its related policy had been the buildup of communities of highly trained professionals in many areas who are indeed vital to growth but who cannot sustain themselves after the sudden cessation of assistance. This fate awaited many intellectuals and professionals in Turkey when assistance agencies withdrew or contracted in the mid-to-late 1960s.

We were told of more than two hundred young Turkish scholars who returned from American graduate training "flying over the clouds," bound that they would reform their system in the image they had come to know and respect. After two decades, they grew tired and discouraged with the prospect of old forces of reaction building up against them once again and no continued reinforcements.

Many Indonesians wondered if the same ultimately discouraging consequences awaited them in the years ahead. One interviewee serenaded us with the refrain "Is there Life after AID?" Evidently he thought not.

It was widely agreed that an appropriate strategy for assistance agencies was to recognize the long-term, continuous nature of growth relationships and to commit themselves to the sustained support required for the permanent establishment of professional or intellectual traditions. In particular, every training project should have an extended "tail" of support to sustain the trainees over their life course.

IV.
The Causes
of Decay

The siren song of administration. The causes of intellectual and professional decay are not always readily distinguishable from the manifestations of it. For example, almost everyone mentions that a "drift into administration" is associated with the phenomenon. But it is unclear whether this drift causes the problem by luring professionals away from pursuit of their subjects or represents a path deliberately chosen by those already decayed scientists and professionals who have lost their touch or, as one person put it, "who have lost their fastball." It is clear that in the countries we visited administration is often a surer route to fame and fortune than the life of the mind is, but this fact still does not answer the question of cause and effect. It does appear, however, that the particular form of decay that occurs with movement into administration is peculiarly irreversible; once across that occupational divide, no man doth return.

There may be a distinctive growth pattern in the early years of many developing countries that helps to explain the flow, sometimes approaching a flood, of professionals and intellectuals into administration. Abrupt decolonization creates one-time demands for middle-level and high-level bureaucrats and executives that tend to drain the rest of the system. During this period, pressures on the professions and disciplines are intense as the administrative temptress lures away their best. In another sense, however, it can be seen that administration affords a safety valve for persons in whom decay has already done its work. Indeed, the availability of numerous administrative opportunities conceals the full breadth of the problem of decay.

One peculiar effect of the attraction of very young professionals to senior administration, some suggested to us, is that they not only lose their skills but also make rather ineffective administrators. By missing the experience of moving through the ranks from junior positions, they are deprived of the part of their lifelong learning that brings maturity and, in the long run, enables them to make coherent, continuing use of the skills they acquired in higher education.

In any event, in many Third World countries the period of acute administrative shortage is coming to a close. Consequently, the lure away from scholarly and professional pursuits, as well as the means for those who have already experienced decay to obtain release from frustration, is nearing an end. To the extent that the administrative shortage wanes, the problem of decay will become even more evident.

Income and demand for skills. Inadequate compensation and support services were invariably among the principal causes of decay observed by us and identified by others. Noncompetitive salaries help to explain the departure of skilled people from disciplines and professions for which they were trained. They also explain low morale, caused when supplementary employment has to be sought: the pressure to seek additional income destroys private life and distracts the professional or intellectual from a chosen career. As one disgruntled Mexican scholar remarked to us, "My kids can't eat books and papers."

In institutional terms, resource constraints mean inadequate libraries, laboratories, computational facilities, and other tools of the trade. Clearly all countries to which the foreign-trained scholars return cannot be expected to supply the same high levels of remuneration and scholarly infrastructure that were on display during their graduate training abroad. Nevertheless, it is important for all concerned to appreciate the fact that without some of these rewards and facilities skills will simply atrophy and disappear.

Another cause mentioned often was faulty information obtained by students planning to study abroad, first about which institutions would best suit their needs and second about which courses of study would be most useful to them after their return. This led to poor planning and faulty program decisions. The problem is greater for the "nonsponsored" student attempting to plan his own higher education and often responding to current American fashion, but it even occurs for some "sponsored" students who receive poor advice.

It is hard to maintain skills even when they are in the highest demand, but when these skills are unwanted their maintenance becomes impossible. An engineering student who masters nuclear or satellite technology only to return home to no reactors and no space program may become so discouraged that he simply abandons the engineering profession entirely.

Language and Culture. Beyond agreement on the overriding importance of adequate resources, opinion is divided about the causes of decay. Among the factors mentioned most often is loss of facility in the use of English, the predominant language of scholarly communication. "When your English gets rusty," one Mexican scientist told us, "you lose confidence about publishing in it. In consequence, you are likely to lose contact with the worldwide community of scholars in your discipline."

The causes of decay seem to be profoundly entwined in the social and political context (the "zeitgeist") of countries in the developing world. One educational leader talked to us worriedly of a "thinness" in the habits and traditions of research, critical appraisal, scientific endeavor, and scholarly writing. This veneer comes under greatest stress for those scholars and scientists who set out not merely to maintain a level of competence but also to push back the frontiers of their subjects. There are often no cultural support systems that stimulate and encourage a young intellectual or professional to stay at the forefront of a discipline or scientific tradition with a global value system, and especially no support system that places a premium on novelty, innovation, and scholarly competition.

In the view of one Turkish sociologist, her country's culture is based on affiliation and friendship. Individualistic and competitive norms are substantially alien. "To be loved is more important than to achieve." Publication in international journals and other manifestations of continued activity at the scholarly threshold are as likely to be perceived as demeaning and threatening to colleagues at home as to be regarded a source of local or national pride. They may also be seen as simply showing off.

Scholars and bureaucrats in all countries observed that relatively automatic promotion systems tend to condition accomplishments, especially research output. In most universities, for example, it is expected that scholars will produce substantial publications as they jump over each of the two or three promotion hurdles through the ranks to full professor. This tradition guarantees several "hiccups" of output during a scholar's career but tends to discourage continued production once the last hurdle has been cleared. In the United States and other Western countries, scholarly productivity is similarly rewarded, and the lack of it penalized, in the early phases of academic careers. It is a costly and inefficient system wherever it exists. A system that rewards performance continuously and fairly over an entire scholarly lifetime seems likely to yield a larger total output. Such a system should in time yield a "research culture" (which we often heard is now lacking).

In the absence of a research culture, the very notion of intellectual refreshment is foreign. As one Turkish scholar described his education in the United States and his return home, "You are taught to swim and then thrown in the pool and expected to swim vigorously for the rest of your life." In the absence of a work ethic and an associated reward system based on productivity, the fact is that intellectual and professional decay is not likely to affect the prospects for career advancement. In consequence, a powerful motive to resist decay is absent.

One indication of a characteristically skeptical attitude toward activity at the scholarly frontier, we were told, is the atmosphere of professional meetings that often degenerate into mere social or political gatherings where "everyone has something to sell." The reward system of the disciplines and professions, moreover, typically reinforces that of individual institutions, placing little weight on innovative contributions. The mere fact of foreign graduate or professional education is often the basis for status and prestige rather than for the continued exercise and improvement of the skills and research capacities acquired through this education. Under these conditions, once a foreign degree has been attained, decay in the content of the knowledge gained has little effect on status or rewards; the label is inviolate. Because decay incurs no penalty, it is more likely to occur.

Authoritarian political and social traditions seem also to be deterrents to intellectual vigor and creativity. In a society where candor is not encouraged in everyday life and where threats to any hierarchy can become personally dangerous, it is doubtful that a free, uninhibited atmosphere of inquiry, which is necessary for the survival of a progressive scientific community and for intellectual advance, can be sustained for long. In the words of one observer-participant, "The commitment to uninhibited inquiry is oxidized most rapidly under a totalitarian regime."

One aspect of life in an authoritarian environment is that scientists and intellectuals may be constrained or prohibited, often frivolously, from applying their skills to problems that they perceive to be either of highest national priority or of exceptional scientific interest but that those in authority judge to be inimical to their interests. These problems may range from humanistic topics, such as questions of historical interpretation, to topics in the physical sciences that impinge on national security. The condition of actual, or implicit, censorship appears to have a concentrated dispiriting result. For a scientist or professional it is catastrophic not to be able to exercise skills, but in the environment of a new nation it is doubly destructive of morale to be compelled to address issues of lesser moment while matters of pressing national concern are addressed by those in positions of political or social privilege. The incentives for those who are out of favor to "keep up" are eroded even more than usual. Regrettably, we found this problem in evidence, in varying degrees, in all three countries we studied.

The characteristic of an authoritarian political regime that is most conducive to the encouragement of intellectual and professional decay is the frequent suppression of reason and criticism through the eccentric political or personal decisions of the ruling authority. Why retain your analytic skills if action will be determined without resorting to analysis? The counterpart to the authoritarian political regime in the private sector is the private or family-owned corporation. There, we were told repeatedly, the professional skills of business management and even of high technology are little valued; hence, their decay is little lamented. However, the opening of a nation's economy to worldwide competition seems to stimulate a Darwinian process: the antiquated family-owned corporation faced with competitors using modern management and techniques simply goes to the wall.

While the aforementioned negative cultural forces operate to keep intellectuals and scientists from sustaining commitment to their disciplines and professions, the rival attractions of old habits, old standards, and old friends also remain strong. It is a highly disciplined, self-confident scholar or professional, indeed, who can swim successfully against this cultural current. The temptation to lie back and float with the current, or to leave the water altogether and find more agreeable bathing elsewhere, is almost irresistible. Still another alternative is to accept fatalistically a derivative role in intellectual affairs and to abandon all hope of retaining a place on the forefront. In the parlance of one Latin American, "Research then becomes 'copy the gringo.'" In this condition of self-induced intellectual dependency, options and opportunities are closed out before they even appear.

To the extent that intellectual and professional decay has cultural causes, prevention must have cultural solutions. Some alternative strategies are discussed below.

Recession and its effects. The causes of decay discussed thus far are continuing ones, or are at least associated with conditions that, as a general rule, may prevail in any developing country. In addition, however, there were peculiar conditions present during the time of our visits that were associated with the economic recession that gripped most of the world during much of the 1970s and early 1980s. Although these conditions can be expected to disappear in the normal course of the business cycle, their effects are none the less severe, and there are indications that in at least some cases they are irreversible.

"Short-term" effects naturally are related largely to temporary resource shortages. The effects occur in several areas. There are declines in compensation for intellectuals and professionals that lead to brain drain, both externally, to other countries, and internally, away from occupations requiring advanced skills and training. (The Mexican universities, for example, reported a significant exodus from their faculties to government and business.) Also, there are reductions in support for research as a result of financial stringency that are important and more complex. In most cases, fewer funds are provided for laboratories, libraries, released time, assistance, and travel. But in addition to these cuts, in response to a sense of national economic crisis, what funds remain for research may be shifted toward short-term, applied, and "practical" goals, which are inimical to the long-term sustenance of the intellectual and professional communities.

During the recent economic hard times associated with wide fluctuations in the prices of energy supplies, most Third World nations have experienced acute shortages of foreign exchange. One understandable response has been to cut out, temporarily at least, what are perceived to be frivolities and seemingly postponable expenses, such as foreign travel, foreign memberships, and purchases of books and periodicals published abroad. The result for the local intellectual and professional elites has been suspension of contact with the life of the international community. There have indeed been drastic cuts in library acquisitions, exchange of personnel, and, of particular importance, overseas postgraduate training of some of the best young minds.

A miscalculation in the tactic of accomplishing short-term adjustments in the balance of payments by severing international intellectual and professional links comes from the belief that the adjustments can easily be compensated for in better times. In Turkey in particular, we heard repeated accounts of how links with American counterparts, built up with great cost and effort only a few years before, were allowed to lapse and seem now beyond recovery. People leave institutions and retire; memories fail; and other opportunities appear. Even the most longstanding relationships, if not carefully nurtured, simply disappear. In all three countries, one of the strongest impressions we took away from our conversations was of the richness and accomplishment of the many international linkages built up over the years, and of their fragility. Failure to sustain a relationship, even over a brief period, may render it irretrievable.

The sudden cessation of foreign graduate training not only cuts off regular infusions of young blood and foreign ideas into the disciplines and professions but also breaks important international transmission belts for information about what is happening on the frontiers of fields. The sense of true panic felt by many academics in reaction to their suddenly straitened circumstances and academic poverty in almost all respects was tangible. One scholar observed, "No secretary, no Xerox, no travel money, no books, no journals, no assistance, no everything. If I lose my international contacts, I'm done."

The deleterious effects on intellectual and professional competence from short-term financial crises are not confined to the academy. In business and government, recession has led to the neglect of certain activities that require employees with the highest skills. Potentially great long-term returns from such activities as product research, corporate planning, and internal retraining are forsaken. Those who have been trained and employed to conduct these activities are laid off or transferred. We did not find adequate appreciation of the potential long-term effects of what were thought of as short-term expediencies in business and government. Distant horizons were ignored in favor of today's or tomorrow's crisis. For the staff formerly involved in the neglected activities, the result is severe career disruption; really interesting problems are abandoned for the merely routine ones.

After the intellectual hiatus brought on by recession, however, it is very difficult, or even impossible, to recapture the momentum of earlier life. As in the case of those engaged in purely scientific pursuits in universities, the decay of skills and competencies caused by temporary interruption of their use can be substantially irreversible for those employed in government and industry. The collapse is especially precipitous in firms, departments, or agencies where a critical mass of highly skilled staff members has not yet been established (as in some analytical units within government and planning departments in business). The decline in foreign investments that typically characterizes a recession helps to accelerate decay. International flows of capital bring with them not only a transfer of new technology but also, indirectly, the means by which technology previously embedded in humans can be maintained. The cessation of flows brings accelerated obsolescence.

Ironically, it must be recorded that recession also appears to have certain countervailing effects on the process of decay. In some cases, both business and government are inspired by the foreign exchange crisis to seek intellectual and professional services at home that had previously been purchased abroad, especially various kinds of research and staff training. In this way a new local market for indigenous intellectual products is developed.

Intellectual and professional fragmentation. A final cause of decay worth noting grows out of the limited interactions between the academic, corporate, and government communities in developing countries. In the increasingly complex setting in which development must take place, no one sector of society has a monopoly on wisdom or advanced techniques for problem solving. Consequently, decay can be averted in part through sustained contact between university scholars and the business community, between private and public sector groups, and between government and the academy. But these interactions are especially weak in developing countries, where truly separate cultures have materialized, where great distrust and ignorance are prevalent in each community in response to the goals and expertise of those in other sectors, and where the prevalent attitude tends to be separation rather than integration. By failing to learn from their counterparts in other types of institutions, many professionals in developing countries are needlessly hampering their ability to stay abreast of their discipline. We discuss this cause further and propose ways to cope with it in the sections on prevention of decay.

V.
The
Countries
Selected

It was no simple task to select the developing countries that would serve as the "data base" for our investigation into the decline of professional competencies. The more than four billion people who reside on this planet are citizens of a wide variety of nation-states numbering in excess of 160. Excluding tiny island and mountain states and assorted other idiosyncratic political entities, there are 126 countries whose economic developments are tabulated routinely by the World Bank. Of these, 19 are classified as "industrial market economies" (the United States, Japan, several members of the Commonwealth, and most West European states), eight are "East European nonmarket economies" (including the Soviet Union), and five are in the special category of "high-income oil exporters" (Saudi Arabia, Libya, and three other Persian Gulf states).

This leaves 94 countries divided into two broad categories, "low-income economies" (34) and "middle-income economies" (the remaining 60). This latter category is in turn divided into two groups, "lower middle-income" and "upper middle-income." Taken overall, therefore, almost half of the world's countries whose economies are significant enough to be followed by the World Bank fall into the middle-income category. This, then, is the classification most representative of the developing countries.

It is obvious, of course, that selecting any set of countries from this category is somewhat arbitrary. Not only are no two countries alike in most essential characteristics — geographical location, topography, culture, history, pattern of economic development, type of political system — but many states are also highly diverse within their own borders. Analysts who take selective samples of such complex societies are perennially vulnerable to the criticism that they have ignored crucial within-country distinctions.

Nonetheless, decisions had to be made and a set of countries had to be selected in order to provide the necessary grist for our analytical mill. In making our selections, we were driven by several key considerations. First, we sought geographical diversity. We had, as was mentioned earlier, been confronted with the concern about intellectual and professional decay in our previous case study of Brazilians who had studied in the United States. We asked ourselves, Is it solely a Brazilian phenomenon? Is it restricted to Latin American states? This seemed highly improbable. Indeed, we were ourselves already painfully aware of the problem in the United States. But how does this phenomenon vary in different geographical and socioeconomic settings? We could only begin to gain an appreciation of the problem, and of how it was being addressed, by casting our geographical net widely.

Second, we decided to select "major" developing countries — states that are reasonably large in area and population. We were fearful that the more esoteric the characteristics of the countries we selected were, the more limited the value of our research findings would be.

Third, we wanted to study the phenomenon in societies that have sent substantial numbers of their youth to the United States to study, especially to study at the graduate level, and whose policies are of significance to the United States. Since our intended audience for this report includes American funding agencies and policymakers concerned with international education, it seemed foolish to choose countries that have negligible contacts with the United States.

Fourth, we deliberately sought diversity and rich experience, in terms of use of international education, among the countries we selected. In order to probe the extent to which intellectual decay is a function of time as well as of circumstance, it was important that we visit countries that have had varied profiles of the number of international students they have sent abroad over the last several decades.*

Fifth, and finally, we were guided by practical considerations of where, given our limited time and resources, we could most likely conduct rich, productive fieldwork. The possibility of assistance from the field offices of the Institute of International Education and the Ford Foundation (with which we have long-standing contacts) were not trivial considerations in our country selection.

These five concerns led us to select Mexico, Indonesia, and Turkey from the category of "middle-income" developing countries.

---

*In the years since 1954–55, there has been considerable change in the proportion of students countries send to attend U.S. colleges and universities. Until 1969–70, the country that sent the most students was Canada. Canada was replaced in 1974–75 by Iran, which kept the lead until 1982–83. Taiwan then assumed the lead. Within Latin America, Colombia, Mexico, and Cuba (twice) were leading countries until 1979–80, when Venezuela took the lead. It has kept the lead ever since. In the Middle East, Iran has always been the leading country, so it is interesting to note which countries have been second over the years: Israel and Turkey alternated until 1979–80, when Saudi Arabia attained the position. In that year, Turkey ceased to be among the five leading Middle Eastern countries, and in 1983–84 Israel was no longer among the leading five. The figures for South and Southeast Asia are somewhat confusing, since until 1964–65 "China," the leading country, included both Taiwan and Hong Kong; "China" led until 1964–65, when India took over. In 1969–70 the lead went to Taiwan: Taiwan has kept it since, except in 1974–75, when Hong Kong had it. Mexico has been among the five leading Latin American countries since 1954–55. Turkey was among the five leading Middle Eastern countries until 1969–70; and Indonesia has never been among the five leading South and Southeast Asian countries.

VI.
Prevention of Decay: Country Profiles and Case Studies

Political Culture and Development

A study of this kind must be much more than an examination of certain patterns embedded in the processes of international education. It is, at the same time, an exploration of political culture and an assessment of the dynamics of political and economic development in highly complex societies.

Two decades ago it was recognized in the scholarly literature that "in order to understand better the dynamics of political development we must make our analyses in terms of the ways in which people develop, maintain, and change the fundamental basis of political behavior, and in terms of the collective stability and instability of different constellations of attitudes and sentiments."[1] In addressing the substantively important but analytically slippery concept of "political culture," it was asserted that "the notion of political culture assumes that the attitudes, sentiments, and cognitions that inform and govern political

[1] Lucian Pye, ed., *Political Culture and Political Development* (Princeton: Princeton University Press, 1965), p. 6.

23

behavior in any society are not just random congeries but represent coherent patterns which fit together and are mutually reinforcing."[2]

Although political culture is difficult to measure and has been the subject of interminable academic debate, anyone who has traveled to, for example, France and Germany would certainly be prepared to testify that he has indeed witnessed two clearly distinct political cultures. Early students of this subject sought to broaden the subfield of political science known as "comparative politics" beyond the somewhat wooden and descriptive study of institutions and policies in countries other than the United States. Concentrating on the **behavior** of key individuals and groups, early students of the phenomenon noted the following:

> The concept of political culture thus suggests that the traditions of a society, the spirit of its public institutions, the passions and the collective reasoning of its citizenry, and the style and operating codes of its leaders are not just random products of historical experience but fit together as a part of a meaningful whole and constitute an intelligible web of relations.[3]

But change in political culture goes hand in hand with the process of political development that is equally pertinent to our study of the decline of professional competencies because decline of competency occurs in a milieu that is heavily conditioned by the society's stage of political development. Unless the societal context is understood, the characteristics of the decay phenomenon itself have little meaning:

> The key elements of political development involve, first, with respect to the population as a whole, a change from widespread subject status to an increasing number of contributing citizens, with an accompanying spread of mass participation, a greater sensitivity to the principles of equality, and a wider acceptance of universalistic laws. Second, with respect to governmental and general systemic performance, political development involves an increase in the capacity of the political system to manage public affairs, control controversy, and cope with popular demands. Finally, with respect to the organization of the polity, political development implies greater structural differentiation, greater functional specificity, and greater integration of all the participating institutions and organizations.[4]

These theoretical constructs are useful guides for placing the data we collected in our three countries into comparative perspective. Mexico, still primarily an agricultural nation that is simultaneously experiencing an extraordinary growth in urban population, has the most highly educated population, the most advanced political development, and, in many ways, the greatest appreciation of the problem of professional decay. Large numbers of Mexicans studied in the United States in previous years, especially in the 1970s, and many of these individuals are now in elite positions in the society. But because of the extreme economic problems of recent years (discussed briefly below), as a general rule funds are simply unavailable to provide the necessary materials, visits, and visitors that are necessary for this educated elite to maintain their skills at world-class levels. Therefore, in Mexico there is at present a striking clash be-

---

[2]Pye, *Political Culture*, p. 7.
[3]Pye, *Political Culture*, p. 7.
[4]Pye, *Political Culture*, p. 13.

tween a well-developed political culture — with increasing citizen participation in civic affairs, a reasonably well-functioning political system that is coping with popular demands, and considerable integration of the participating institutions and organizations — and a sudden inability to meet the economic, educational, and professional needs of a society that until very recently was extraordinarily optimistic about its future.

In Turkey, by contrast, there is a pattern of political culture and development marked more by successes of the distant past than by ones in recent times. Turkey is ranked second among the three countries in many indicators of political and economic development (in urbanization, for example, according to World Bank statistics for 1982, 44 percent of Turkish citizens lived in urban areas compared to 68 percent in Mexico and 22 percent in Indonesia). It is a nation-state with a glorious past and an uncertain future whose historical contrasts are mirrored in our study of decay. Large numbers of Turkish citizens studied abroad during the 1960s (as described below), but over the last 15 years a variety of circumstances kept Turkey turned inward. The political system essentially broke down in the late 1970s and completely lost its ability to cope with popular demands. Turkey has been trying to recover ever since but confronts such enormous political and economic challenges that the retardation of professional and intellectual decay cannot, at present, find its way onto the priority list of governmental and educational institutions. The country's principal challenge is to rejuvenate its once proud and productive institutions. Decay prevention can apparently be addressed only when tangible progress has been made on this more fundamental level.

Indonesia fits most easily into the general American perception of a developing country striving to reach ever-increasing heights of economic and political development. Of the three countries, it has the lowest level of citizen awareness of the principles of equality, a still-limited capacity for the political system to control controversy (as exemplified by its problems with civil strife cited below), and only a moderate degree of structural differentiation. Indonesia is in the midst of a period of intense social change in which the predominantly rural population is becoming acquainted with the promises and trappings of modern life through rural broadcasting, agricultural extension workers, and other channels. Consequently, new values and ideas are being spread throughout the society, in both urban and rural settings. In this societal context, slowly but steadily increasing numbers of individuals are being sent abroad to study. The initial wave sent in the 1950s and 1960s returned to build the basic institutions of postcolonial Indonesia. Now the next generation will be expected to make contributions on the frontiers of their disciplines and must therefore guard against problems of intellectual and professional decay. The subject of our study, therefore, is now first emerging as an issue in Indonesia.

To reiterate, we have invoked some general notions of political culture and political development primarily to remind the reader that there is extraordinary diversity among the developing countries and that what is found to be prevalent in one society may be entirely irrelevant in another. It is particularly important to appreciate this diversity when considering the implementation of specific recommendations for the retardation of the decay process. We seek merely to emphasize the need to be sensitive to these cultural and political constraints both in evaluating the dynamic quality of developing countries and in proposing recommendations to improve their societal performance.

The Cases and Their Significance

We shall now briefly review the major characteristics of each of the countries we visited and the cases we identified in which efforts to maintain professional competencies were reaping tangible benefits.

The cases describe programs, in the United States as well as in the three countries, that seem to us to respond in various ways to the phenomenon of decay. Only brief descriptions of these cases are presented, with those features that are most directly relevant to our present concern emphasized. We make little attempt to evaluate the programs, although obviously our selection implies our sense of their positive value. We should emphasize that very few of these programs were created, or are now operated, for the purpose of resisting or correcting intellectual and professional decay. They all have other, usually multiple, purposes.

Our intent in setting forth these cases is twofold. The first is to stimulate policymakers in all countries to reflect on whether or not these models can usefully be replicated or adapted in their own countries. We try to provide enough detail to initiate this process of reflection. Obviously anyone wishing to pursue a model further than its description here should contact the principals directly. The second intent in presenting these cases is to encourage appreciation of the programs' decay-fighting accomplishments. We suggest that they and other programs like them should be scrutinized carefully by their actual and potential sponsors to ascertain their full overall social value; when they are weighed in the balance, this function of decay prevention should be given full credit.

Note that the individual cases can be interpreted in one of several ways. A few of them, especially the U.S. cases, are of programs established explicitly to improve the intellectual and professional competencies of developing-country students who have studied in the United States. Others are programs that, though they have not in the past been used to maintain the skills of individuals trained abroad, may well be used or adapted for this purpose. Still others, such as the corporate-sponsored programs, illustrate approaches within developing countries to maintain international standards in various fields. Finally, overall the cases demonstrate an awareness within developing countries of the need to maintain skills through continuing education in order not to lose competitive advantages.

Mexico

Mexico, with an estimated population in 1984 in excess of 76 million, is that huge country "south of the border" that is now reappearing in the American consciousness after more than a half century of neglect. With a GNP per capita in 1982 of $2,270, it ranks in the midrange of the "upper middle-income" category. Based on this measure, it is the richest of the three countries we visited.

Burdened by a foreign debt of approximately $96 billion, Mexico is seeking to recover from decisions made in the 1970s' heady days of rapidly rising oil prices and implementation of a debt-financed strategy for economic growth. With the softness of the oil market in the early 1980s as an inescapable reality, Mexico has had to accept major currency devaluations and other bitter economic medicine in order to survive economically.

Mexicans have long had love-hate feelings toward the United States. They admire American technology, know-how, and productivity, but they deeply resent what they see as the acts of American imperialism in the nineteenth century that stripped them of roughly half their land. Today the pace of Mexican debt repayment and the magnitude of illegal Mexican immigration into the United States, of drug traffic across the Mexican-American border, and of fears in Mexico City of a growing militarization of the United States' Latin American policies, especially with respect to Central America, provide reasons for major policy differences between the two governments.

It has been suggested that Mexico is an example of "an established revolution," in which authority has been concentrated in a single dominant political movement — a revolutionary party, the PRI, that has controlled the levers of power in Mexican society since 1917.[5] Although modern Mexico has experienced many political twists and turns since the revolution, the following major characteristics continue to predominate: the existence of a tolerated opposition, although its influence is deliberately circumscribed; an absence of hostilities along linguistic, ethnic, or religious lines; the maintenance of peasant support for the party through a policy of land reform carried out under PRI auspices; the tying of the organized urban masses to the party through a generally prolabor policy; a relatively nondoctrinaire approach to economic development that has permitted the emergence of a powerful private sector coexisting with the growth of the public sector; a small, professionalized, politically neutralized military force; continued problems of graft and corruption at various levels in the political system; an adherence to the doctrine of "no reelection," in which the president serves a single six-year term; and a historical experience marked more by political development than by economic or social development.[6]

In Mexico education is free and compulsory, providing for two years of preprimary, six years of primary, and three years of secondary training. At the primary level, roughly 75 percent of the schools are located in rural areas and are public institutions. Most of the remaining private schools are run by religious orders. At the postsecondary level, Mexico boasts more than 35 universities and colleges. The two largest institutions of higher education, the Universidad Nacional Autonoma de Mexico (the Autonomous National University of Mexico) and the Instituto Politecnico Nacional (National Polytechnic Institute), are located in Mexico City.

In recent years Mexico has made substantial strides in the education of its population. According to statistics in the *World Development Report 1984* (p. 267), in 1981, 15 percent of the population aged 20–24 was enrolled in higher

[5]Robert E. Scott, "Mexico: The Established Revolution," in *Political Culture and Political Development*, ed. Lucian Pye (Princeton: Princeton University Press, 1965), pp. 330–395. (See also L. Vincent Padgett, *The Mexican Political System, Second Edition* (Boston: Houghton Mifflin, 1976).)
[6]Martin C. Needler, *Politics and Society in Mexico* (Albuquerque: University of New Mexico Press, 1971), pp. 105–117.

education compared to only 3 percent for the same age group in 1960. This is by far the largest percentage, as well as the largest percentage increase, of the three countries studied. Statistical comparisons at the secondary and primary levels, fte that Mexico has a substantially better educated population than either Turkey or Indonesia.

One of the consequences of the recent downturn in the Mexican economy is that funds have been greatly reduced for foreign study, book purchases, foreign visitors, and travel abroad, all tending to exacerbate the problem of maintaining professional competencies. Nonetheless, in 1983 there were still more than 1,100 Mexican graduate students in the United States, with approximately 33 percent studying engineering and the physical sciences, 18 percent enrolled in business and management programs, and 13 percent in agricultural studies. There were more graduate students from Mexico in the United States that year than from any other Latin American country. In addition, at the undergraduate level, there were 1,200 Mexicans enrolled, compared to 1,600 Colombians and more than 5,000 Venezuelans.[7]

In the course of our travels, we encountered several interesting examples of programs to maintain skill levels that involved governmental institutions, academia, and the private sector. They are described in the following pages.

Mexican Cases

1. IPADE

IPADE — the Instituto Panamericano de Alta Direccion de Empresa — is a privately funded graduate school of business and management located in an old, sprawling, charming hacienda in the southern part of Mexico City. IPADE was founded in 1967 with the assistance of several faculty members and administrators from the Harvard Graduate School of Business Administration (HBS) and the Instituto de Estudios Superiores de la Empresa (IESE) in Barcelona, Spain. Many of its programs are modeled aftr those of HBS and the IESE, and faculty members from both institutions continue to play an advisory role in the life of IPADE.

IPADE's background is especially significant from our perspective because the HBS in particular prides itself on its varied offerings of midcareer and executive training programs. There seems little doubt that this lifelong learning philosophy, even — perhaps especially — for top management, has been embraced by IPADE. This is in sharp contrast to the notion we encountered frequently in our travels that management skills, once acquired at home or abroad, will serve for a lifetime. IPADE clearly rejects this notion.

It is also worth noting IPADE's clear commitment to public welfare as well as to private profit. Its formal statement of purpose asserts that "The constant growth of a nation (and of a company as well) involves a good deal of long-term economic and social planning which, in turn, requires discipline and organization — and, of course, great dedication — this being particularly true in the lesser developed countries." Through its programs for training, retraining, and

---

[7]Institute of International Education, *Open Doors: 1983/84* (New York: Institute of International Education, 1984).

refreshment, IPADE commits itself to the development and preservation of planning capacity in Mexico's business elite.

IPADE offers an "exclusive" master of business administration (MBA) program to which it admits 65 carefully selected students each year. As at the HBS, virtually all instruction at IPADE is through the case method. Here the pedagogical approach is not to learn management theory and apply it deductively but to understand particular real-world business and management problems and to derive inductively some general lessons from them. Approximately half the cases used at IPADE are generated by the faculty, drawn from their analyses of experiences in the Mexican business community. The other half are Spanish translations of HBS cases.

In addition to the master's degree program, IPADE provides the Mexican business community with opportunities for continuing education. This is accomplished by offering on a permanent basis three nondegree short courses that are conducted in Spanish. The first, the Program of High Direction, is carried out over 32 weeks and is geared to top-level business managers. The second, the Program of Direction, is addressed to lower-level business managers and lasts 28 weeks. Finally, the Program of Continuity and Current Affairs is specifically designed to refresh the knowledge of those who have taken any of IPADE's courses after they have been out in the business world for several years. Moreover, IPADE also has a permanent program of guest lecturers that complements the basic programs; most of the lecturers come from the Mexican private and public sectors.

In order to give some detailed sense of the programs of lifelong learning offered by IPADE, the official descriptions of two of them follow:

AD2 — Advanced Management Program (begun in 1967)

This program has been conceived for the benefit of the highest level executives. To be eligible, the prospective participant to the course must prove he has performed the duties of a top executive officer for a period of at least five years or its equivalent in the judgment of the School.

It should be emphasized here that the whole concept of IPADE is founded on the principle that the man is more important than any management techniques. Therefore, during the eight months of the Program (from October to May, one day per week, Thursday afternoons and Friday mornings), the participant will be involved — really submerged — in the critical analysis of concrete and realistic situations which a company usually has to face from day to day. This is done both in small teams and in plenary sessions, with the deliberate purpose of assisting the participant in increasing and improving his aptitudes and skills in the formulation of policies and decisions.

The interchange of ideas, experiences, and conclusions — resulting from the participation of an average of eighty executives per class — offers great possibilities for the enrichment of their professional and personal development.

This method of teaching, which implies the analysis and synthesis of concrete cases, leads the participant to the thorough comprehension and conscientious solution of specific problems related to the major operating areas of a business: marketing; production; finance; operations management; corporate policy; human behavior; personnel selection, planning, and development; planning and control; and analysis of the economic, social, and political environment.

Refresher and Continuity Programs (begun in 1968)

Within the framework of its institutional objectives, IPADE offers special "continuity courses" to its former participants and alumni from its Advanced Management, Management Development, and Master's Programs. These continuity courses are actually an extension and complementary to the basic programs since they constitute an uninterrupted cycle of instruction planned year after year. They are offered with characteristics specifically applicable to each of the basic programs, normally through eight sessions — one per month from October through May — that represent an unbeatable opportunity to meet the challenge of the times and to keep posted on the most recent advances and achievements in the art and science of business management.

IPADE sees itself as training Mexico's business leaders of both today and tomorrow. This function is carried out with a small faculty — 22 full-time professors and 13 part-time instructors — most of whom received graduate training abroad (primarily in the United States). The faculty for the most part were themselves students of the case method and find it relatively easy to adapt this approach to the study of the private sector in Mexico. More like the HBS than many other American business schools, IPADE has a faculty that is primarily involved in teaching, case writing, and consulting — all of which are interrelated — rather than in conducting original research and publishing major contributions to the professional literature.

IPADE's institutional strategy is to remain closely associated with the industrial sector. Mexico is a country still marked by major cleavages between government and the private sector. There is relatively little contact between the two, and a good deal of mutual mistrust continues to be the order of the day. In this political-economic climate, IPADE has not sought to train government officials and other nonprofit managers. Rather, it obtains funding and recruits students from the private sector and places most of its graduates in profit-making organizations. IPADE's graduates can count on six or seven job offers each, even in difficult economic times in Mexico. An IPADE degree or association carries a great deal of prestige, since most Mexican business leaders have attended the institution in one capacity or another.

IPADE's curriculum remains oriented toward Mexican business problems. Consequently, the institution is only now beginning to develop instruction in high-tech computing systems and has not yet felt the need to introduce instruction in sophisticated production methods that, like computer-aided design/computer-aided manufacturing (CAD/CAM), we were told, are largely irrelevant to contemporary Mexican industrial concerns. Instead, the focus is on the more well-established manufacturing techniques that are the backbone of Mexican industry.

IPADE has branched out geographically from Mexico City in recent years and has established satellite programs in Guadalajara in the west and Monterrey in the northeast. It prides itself on the strong interaction between its MBA programs and its continuing education programs. An elaborate, up-to-date alumni network helps to facilitate these interactions.

IPADE serves an additional function as a center where Mexico's top business leaders can come together to discuss the basic trends and issues of industrial policy. Presumably, major economic and political issues of the day are also addressed, although on a more informal basis. There are therefore many valuable, but intangible, professional and social connections fostered and maintained by IPADE that transcend the institution's formal training programs and course offerings. The strong alumni ties are reinforced by the relative homogeneity of outlook present in both the political orientation and religious ties of its graduates. IPADE fosters conservative social, political, and economic values that provide additional bonds among those associated with the institution. In this sense, too, it bears considerable resemblance to some of the multifarious functions carried out by the Harvard Business School.

Because of the institution's independence from government control and its substantial support from the private sector, none of the constraints that burden Mexico's public institutions are readily apparent: library and research materials are plentiful; faculty travel, both foreign and domestic, is readily supported; and visitors from the HBS and other U.S. business schools and corporations are routinely invited to lecture. It would appear that a version of "joint research" is carried out between IPADE and the HBS as well. There is sufficient interaction between the two institutions to allow IPADE faculty to stay abreast of the latest cases and management teaching techniques conducted at Harvard, while selected Harvard faculty have an opportunity to observe management practices and the teaching of management in a major developing country.

Clearly the strength and success of IPADE rest on the prior establishment of a vibrant, far-sighted private sector that is relatively free of interference from the central government. These are highly unusual characteristics for a developing country. Therefore, the IPADE model may well have only limited and specialized applicability in many areas of Asia, Africa, and Latin America. IPADE is worth close examination, nevertheless, by policymakers in either the private sector or public sector of a developing country because it is a successful indigenous institution committed to the lifelong refreshment of a crucial element of the nation's elite.

Note the multiplicity of connections, real and potential, between IPADE's programs and our concern with professional decay. Its faculty, most of whom received graduate training in the United States, stay abreast of their own fields in part through constant contact with the Harvard Business School and the use and adaptation of HBS cases for teaching purposes. The students, some of whom have studied in the U.S. and many of whom have increasing professional contacts with Americans and American business, can maintain their competencies by taking advantage of IPADE's numerous executive and continuing education programs. And, potentially, other Mexicans who studied business, economics, management, and related subjects in the United States at one time or another can seek out IPADE as a means of keeping current in their individual fields of specialization.

2. ITAM

ITAM—Instituto Technologico Autonomo de Mexico—is a well-established, privately funded institute located in a handsome set of buildings in Mexico City. ITAM was founded in 1946 and was geared from its inception to the training of students in economics, business, and accounting. Faculties in these three areas were quickly established and remained the backbone of the institution until 1970. Since then ITAM has sought to broaden its programs of instruction and has created new faculties in mathematics, social science, law, and, most recently (1983), computer science. It currently offers baccalaureates of arts (Licenciatura) in all these areas and master's degrees in business administration and economics. ITAM has a faculty of 66 full-time members, most of whom studied at the graduate level in the United States. Its specialized libraries contain some 60,000 volumes and more than 600 periodicals.

In addition, ITAM has made an effort to develop links with major institutions in and outside of Mexico. Its faculty have conducted research for the World Bank with faculty at Princeton University on the political economy of income distribution, with faculty at MIT on energy use and demand in Mexico, and with private firms in Mexico and abroad. Such active research projects clearly have numerous benefits. They no doubt keep ITAM's participating faculty in the forefront of their respective fields. This added knowledge is then reflected in classroom instruction, thereby raising the level of material conveyed to ITAM's students. Moreover, the projects generate income — sometimes for the institution, sometimes for the individual faculty members. Finally, they lend prestige to ITAM within Mexican society, thereby strengthening fund-raising efforts, student and faculty recruitment, and student placement.

ITAM conducts a wide variety of continuing education programs and grants 14 different diplomas beyond the baccalaureate degree. Specialized courses on topics such as finance, applied statistics, and advanced computer systems last an average of 30 weeks. Overall, if IPADE concentrates on top management, ITAM focuses on the middle manager.

Reflecting Mexico's general demographic composition, ITAM's faculty are quite young. Many are in the 35-to-45 age range. Most hold M.A.'s from major American universities, including Michigan, Wisconsin, Columbia, and Chicago, and are in considerable demand for consulting assignments due to ITAM's prestige in Mexico. Some, by their own admission, are now facing serious problems of intellectual and professional decay, in part because they lack sufficient external stimuli. ITAM offers them six-month sabbaticals every six years, so that they can study abroad and acquaint themselves with the latest developments in their respective fields.

It appears, however, that the professional incentives for ITAM's faculty to complete their doctoral studies are not strong. Faculty members can be promoted to top ranks without a doctorate; thus, many may not have engaged in any major independent research projects of the magnitude of a doctoral dissertation. What the faculty need, they claim, is more sustained interaction with senior faculty from the United States and elsewhere. American faculty are needed on-site to carry out joint research and to instruct, formally or informally, the ITAM faculty and students. Mexico's deepening economic difficulties seem to have had a substantially deleterious impact on ITAM's travel and resources budget, unlike the impact on IPADE's.

ITAM seems to us to constitute a major national resource for technological research and training built up at great cost in the postwar years with vision and imagination, but now in danger of rapid deterioration. It is in a particularly precarious condition because of the all-but-dissertation status of many faculty and their need for continual stimulation and intellectual refreshment. It represents what may occur in the institutions of many other developing countries in the years just ahead. Yet, ITAM also represents an opportunity for assistance. Its infrastructure seems ample and solid and its condition subject to recovery. Like IPADE, ITAM has a set of real and potential connections to the issue of decay prevention. Its faculty, most trained in the United States, could stay more current in their fields by enhanced contact from abroad through visitors and joint research activities similar to those presently being undertaken. Faculty with such contacts, in turn, could impart to their students a greater appreciation of the state-of-the-art developments in their fields. And, although at present most of these students are or aspire to be middle managers with limited contacts outside Mexico, there is nothing to prevent ITAM from adapting its programs to the large numbers of Mexican students who have already studied in the United States and other foreign countries and who wish to maintain their skills in the increasingly competitive Mexican and world economies.

3. Justo Sierra Program

Given the major split between the public and private sectors in Mexico and the sense of the need to "choose sides" that seemed prevalent among the major educational institutions in the country, we were pleasantly surprised to learn of the existence of a program designed to bridge these sectoral chasms. The Justo Sierra Program was started as an experimental project by the National University of Mexico (UNAM) in 1982. In December 1983 it was transformed into a formal program of the university under the administrative direction of the coordinator of the humanities. It now claims its own facilities, located downtown in the Zocalo district of Mexico City.

The origins of the program reflect some of the peculiarities that have a special meaning for the problem of intellectual and professional decay in developing countries. It was created amid an atmosphere of new alternatives for the development of Mexico that emerged as a result of the economic potential generated by the revival of the national oil industry in the late 1970s. It was the opinion of some members of UNAM's academic community that the university should be an active participant in the national debate on perspectives of development that was then taking place in the country. Thus, the original intention of the program was to provide members of UNAM's faculty with an opportunity to conduct research on topics related to the "new national challenges" and simultaneously to develop fresh channels of communication between the academic community and the government.

To reach these goals, programs were created in five different areas: urban, regional, and ecological studies; economic studies; political studies; oil and energy problems; and information and computer systems. A strong emphasis on multidisciplinary teams has ensured substantial coordination between these five areas. Among the research projects that the Justo Sierra Program has initiated are "Analysis of the Current Economic Policy on Unemployment and Balance of Trade"; "The Transportation System and its Regional Impact in Mexico"; "Authoritarianism, Elections, and Democracy in Mexico"; "Oil and Public Debt"; and "National Policies of Information."

Since a major purpose of the program is to strengthen ties between the university and government communities, a flexible structure that includes not only research projects but also teaching programs, extension courses, and seminars has been adopted. The program has been very active in organizing conferences and informal meetings that foster debate between academic specialists and government officials. Some of the topics that have been addressed at these meetings are "Technology Development and Rural Economy in Mexico"; "Oil: The International Market and Its Options"; "Ecology and Development in Mexico"; "Energy Policy"; and "Mexico and the United States."

The program also has plans to publish in Mexico, through either UNAM or private publishing companies, the results of some of its research projects and compilations of papers and debates from the events it organizes.

Although much of the program planning is conducted on the UNAM campus, which is far from the city center, the program's downtown location provides government officials with easy access to Justo Sierra meetings. Since Mexico City, with its population in excess of 14 million, is perhaps the most populous and sprawling city in the world, this is an important consideration.

It should be added that since the program is also designed to foster communication among individuals who would normally not interact with each other often, not all the sessions have an academic character. Meetings that have had a decidedly practical and indeed operational orientation have been held to discuss international commercial negotiations, the political and economic dimensions of urban problems, negotiating strategies with the International Monetary Fund, and the connection between microcomputers and public policy. The program is constructed around eight to ten permanent members.

The reaction of government officials to these sessions, we were told, is highly positive because they are hungry to develop the depth of understanding and the skills required for fast reaction to immediate problems. Though some programs have not been successful because of bureaucratic difficulties and sensitivities, most sessions have apparently been well received. They are "organized from within," participation is by invitation only, and discussion is said to be remarkably candid.

The Sierra Program remains funded primarily by UNAM, with limited additional direct government support. Its first director, Marguerita Almada, is a senior and well-respected figure in information sciences. From UNAM's perspective, this program is an effort to "modernize the university from without, not from within." Additional funds from private foundations are required if it is to expand its activities significantly. There is also some question of how to provide incentives so that key figures in the private sector will participate as well.

The very existence of this program is highly noteworthy. Mexico, like many developing and developed countries, is finding that in today's complex technological age, the firm separation of academic, government, and business sectors is a major impediment to efficient and effective use of scarce intellectual resources. Finding clever and subtle ways to expose individuals from each sector to the perspectives and problems of the other sectors is a necessary first step in the process of breaking down these sectoral barriers.

A frequent complaint we heard from professionals and intellectuals was that they had too few opportunities to apply their skills to problems of urgent national concern. In the consequent state of frustration and discouragement, they were especially susceptible to decay. In the developed countries a variety of structures and institutions, including advisory councils and public policy research institutes, constitute the nexus between academe and the policy world and embue the participants with a sense of true and valuable involvement. The Justo Sierra Program is an imaginative and suggestive innovation in this genre that deserves careful study throughout the developing world.

One additional characteristic that the Justo Sierra Program, and others like it, could adopt would be the systematic examination of new developments in various disciplines and their relevance for the nation. Many of the top leaders from government, industry, and academia who would participate in this program would have studied at one time or another in the United States and would continue to maintain contacts with leading figures abroad in their respective fields. It would therefore be possible to use the program not only as a communications link across sectors but also as a collective discussion group and tutorial to promote participant awareness of recent disciplinary advances, which could itself retard the decay process.

4. Monterrey Technical Institute

Monterrey Technical Institute (MTI) is often referred to as "the MIT of Mexico." In reality, however, it has been primarily a teaching institution until relatively recently and only now is vastly expanding its research and continuing education functions.

More than 50 percent of the MTI faculty have had some degree of "upgrading" in the form of graduate study in the United States. It is felt that this refreshment not only reeducates the faculty but also restrains the ill effects of "inbreeding" and encourages varied perspectives toward particular problems and disciplines. This is an especially significant concern for an institution that finds it necessary to hire primarily its own graduates.

The administration of MTI is aware of the need for a critical mass to conduct serious research, and faculty are often provided summer support to further their individual studies. Whereas the dominant mode of research not many years ago was to "copy the gringo," today the faculty are striking out independently in many directions. Virtually all the institute's faculty are now "computer literate" and effectively using their computer skills in research projects that are especially appropriate within the Mexican technological context.

According to MTI administrators, incentives are needed to keep the faculty on top in their fields because tenure is granted after only one year of service. One device is to promote connections with local industry. Roughly 60 percent of the faculty now participate in "practical schools." Each faculty member directs eight to 12 students in an industrial project. In this process everyone gains. The industry acquires cheap, skilled, highly energetic labor. The student gets the taste of a real-world project and is provided with the opportunity to develop the connections that could lead to a permanent position upon graduation. The faculty member earns extra income, becomes acquainted with industry's concerns, and is able to plow new knowledge back into the classroom. Cooperation of this sort may seem painfully difficult for developing countries with scarce intellectual resources, but its novelty should be emphasized for that reason.

These practical schools have been especially successful in chemical engineering and computer science. In most cases the focus is on medium- and long-term problems, such as software development. Individual projects are jointly designed by institute and industry participants and are carried out on industrial sites. Not only does the payoff of the practical schools include student placement, solution of company problems, enhanced faculty experience, and supplemental income, but it also leads to increased institute income and sometimes to the construction of case materials that can be used in courses of instruction.

As at most institutions of higher learning in Mexico, the majority of the faculty members at MTI hold master's degrees (45 percent) while a significantly smaller percentage hold doctorates (15 percent). The objective of the institute is to work on technological problems present in the Mexican environment. Nonetheless, the absence of doctoral-level research experience, which does not always exist in other developing countries (for example, in Indonesia and Turkey), may well limit the ability of the faculty and of the institution to compete at the frontiers of their disciplines. This constraint is also an impediment to the strengthening of academic and business ties in Mexico.

In the course of our interviews, we met many Mexicans in the private sector who had received advanced degrees in technical subjects at top-rated American institutions. When these individuals need research and consulting talent in their corporate capacities, they are far more likely to reach across the border to the United States (if they can afford it), oftentimes to their alma maters, than to seek out local talent. They are just that much more confident that the American faculty member, with his Ph.D. and international reputation, has the skills they need and the ability to deliver promptly the product or service they want than they are that his Mexican academic counterpart does.

In part to overcome some of this inherent skepticism toward the value of local talent, the institute has in recent years adopted an innovative marketing approach. It has developed planning software and data-based management systems that it is trying to sell in the United States. In short, it seeks to establish credibility at home by first gaining a reputation abroad. The institute was described to us as "an extraordinarily entrepreneurial institution." This orientation is in itself a path to sustaining intellectual and professional competence.

As an institution that did not originate in the nation's capital, MTI has placed special emphasis on developing higher education in outlying Mexican provinces. It currently has branches in numerous Mexican cities, including Queretaro, Chihuahua, and Irapuato. This is significant because many developing countries, including Mexico, have a deep-rooted tradition of political, economic, and cultural centralization in the national capital. Efforts to create such institutions in the provinces broaden the range of opportunities for Mexicans who return home after having studied abroad.

MTI is well positioned to address the decay problem in outlying areas. Not all of the Mexicans trained in the United States in recent years reside in Mexico City, and it is even more difficult for those who reside in provincial areas to maintain their skill levels. Through marketing and other ventures in the United States, MTI faculty are able to return to these outlying sections to bring foreign-trained Mexicans up-to-date on the latest developments in their respective fields. In a country where urban centers are growing extremely rapidly, this "outreach" function for decay prevention is especially noteworthy; it might be emulated in other societies with similar success.

At various times our Mexican interviewees told us that in Mexico it continues to be more important to "know who" than to "know how." The private sector is distant from the center of political power, and the country has therefore been described as having an "ideological center" and a "practical frontier." To overcome the prevailing orthodoxy that "whatever is foreign is better than ours," programs must be implemented that reinforce a meritocracy. It is against this cultural context that MTI and other Mexican institutions must struggle to sustain the competencies of their intellectuals and professionals.

Indonesia

Indonesia is the most populous and the poorest of the three countries in our study. With a population well in excess of 150 million, it ranks fifth in the world, after China, India, the Soviet Union, and the United States. Its GNP per capita of $572 in 1982 places it near the bottom of the "lower middle-income" category.

Although the Indonesian population is spread over 13,000 islands in a huge archipelago off the coast of Southeast Asia, roughly two-thirds of the population live on seven percent of the land, the island of Java, "where the Javanese elaborated over centuries a rich culture that has become the single greatest source of Indonesian identity."[8] Indeed, the Indonesian government, with assistance from the World Bank, has been engaged in a transmigration program designed to spread population more evenly. The stated goal is to move about 13 million families from Java to other islands over a 20-year period. In recent years, the government has been able to relocate roughly 100,000 families per year with considerable alleviation of poverty as the primary consequence.[9]

Indonesia gained independence from the Dutch in 1948 after several centuries of colonial rule and a bloody revolutionary war. President Sukarno, a war hero, governed the country from 1948 to 1965. In the last several years of his rule, he moved ideologically toward the People's Republic of China and encouraged the strengthening of the Indonesian Communist Party. The Communists then attempted a coup d'etat and were put down in a brutal countercoup by the Indonesian army led by General Suharto. Suharto took the reins of power, which he still holds today; Sukarno was eased into political oblivion; and huge numbers of alleged Communists, perhaps one million, including many ethnic Chinese, lost their lives. Since the countercoup, Suharto's administration has been marked for the most part by political stability, some economic progress, and a nonaligned foreign policy.

Indonesia is a major oil producer (revenue has increased ninefold since 1965), a member of OPEC, and also a leading member of the Association of Southeast Asian Nations (ASEAN). It has large deposits of tin, nickel, copper, and bauxite and huge quantities of rubber and timber. The military government has encouraged extensive foreign investment in the country, and it has been estimated that one-third of all foreign industrial investment is American.

The religious preference of Indonesians is overwhelmingly Muslim (estimated at more than 80 percent of the population), but ethnic cleavages constantly tug at the fabric of Indonesian society. In 1985 the government was

---

[8]Donald K. Emerson, *Indonesia's Elite: Political Culture and Cultural Politics* (Ithaca: Cornell University Press, 1976), p. 20.
[9]The World Bank, *World Development Report 1984* (New York: Oxford University Press, 1985), p. 99.

confronted by armed rebellions in Irian Jaya in the far east of the archipelago and in the Moluccas. Relations with Australia have worsened because of atrocities said to have been committed by Indonesian forces in these areas. Moreover, the Suharto regime is concerned about the military threat posed by Vietnam in Southeast Asia and the growing ties between the United States and the People's Republic of China. There is tangible concern in Jakarta that the ethnic Chinese in Indonesia, aided and abetted by the PRC, may once again threaten the regime. Political instability in the Philippines, another ASEAN member, is also a potential problem for the Suharto government, which is closely monitoring the American role in that tormented country.

Educational opportunities for Indonesians have increased substantially since independence. Whereas the Dutch made little effort to educate the indigenous Indonesian population, under Presidents Sukarno and Suharto, respectively, the emphasis has been placed on mass education. This emphasis reaped considerable benefits; by the early 1970s, it was estimated that about 40 percent of the population over the age of 10 was literate. By the mid-1970s there were more than 40 public universities in the country and more than 200 private institutions of higher learning. The present educational program, administered by the Ministry of Education and Culture, calls for six years of primary, three years of junior secondary, and three years of senior secondary education.

In the early 1970s the Ministry of Education and Culture established consortia in five fields — agriculture, science and technology, medicine, social sciences, and education — to maintain standards in the Indonesian university system. Postgraduate programs were to be concentrated in several target institutions, each of which was to receive additional budgetary support to upgrade the quality of faculty and facilities. What we in the United States would characterize as "centers of excellence" were to be created at the Institut Pertanian Bogor (Bogor Agricultural Institute); the Institut Teknologi Bandung (Bandung Institute of Technology); the Universitas Indonesia (in Jakarta); Gadjah Mada University (in Jogjakarta); and the Universitas Airlangga (in Surabaja).

Nonetheless, because of rapid population growth, Indonesia has, in percentage terms, failed to make great strides in education at the postsecondary level. According to World Bank statistics, in 1981 only 3 percent of the population aged 20–24 were enrolled in programs of higher education, an increase from 1 percent in 1960. This places Indonesia third in terms of educated population among the three countries studied.

Relatively few Indonesians are presently studying in the United States (in 1984–85 there were 7,190 Indonesian students at U.S. institutions), although the numbers are increasing. Figures place Indonesia behind Taiwan, Malaysia, and Hong Kong among Southeast Asian states that send students to the United States. Given the present stage of Indonesian economic and political development, it is not surprising that the cases we identified for maintaining skills and competencies draw heavily on foreign — that is, non-Indonesian — involvement. Although relatively few Indonesians have studied abroad, the ones who have have typically risen to prominent positions. Several members of the cabinet, as well as many others at senior levels of government, hold advanced degrees from distinguished American universities. Recently, for example, the Foreign Minister, Yale University Law School graduate Mochtar Kusumaatmadja, was noted in the American press for his efforts to assist the U.S. government with efforts to locate American servicemen missing in Vietnam.

Indonesian Cases

1. Citicorp/Indonesia Training Program
Some of the most knowledgeable and active participants in midcareer training are the major multinational corporations and international banks that realize that maintaining skills and acquiring new ones are requirements for being effective in a highly competitive environment. A particularly impressive program is conducted at Citicorp/Indonesia headquarters in a modern high-rise building in the center of Jakarta.

Citicorp, of course, is a major international banking operation with some 70,000 employees, of whom 5,000 are at or above the vice-president level. In Jakarta, virtually all personnel other than senior bank representatives are Indonesian nationals. Each employee of the bank receives five to ten days per year of "exceptional training," which consists mainly of sessions conducted through Citicorp's corporate lending department. Sessions involve formal classroom learning on such topics as credit analysis, advanced lending strategy, and advanced account management. Lectures are given, readings are assigned, and examinations are conducted. Most of the sessions are held in Jakarta, but some specialized, more advanced courses are offered at Citicorp's Asian training center in Manila.

There are several incentives for employees to participate in these training courses. First, the corporate ethos, in which constant training and refreshment is the norm, seems to produce peer pressure. Failure to attend five to ten days of retraining each year is to buck the trend in the bank. Second, at salary review time, attendance at and performance in these courses are said to be weighed heavily by senior management. Third, significant career promotions are tied to these training sessions. The sessions provide an opportunity for employees to demonstrate technical, specialized proficiencies; to meet with peers from other branches of the bank; to catch the attention of senior bank personnel; and to gain the skills necessary for movement to the next level of seniority. In the bank environment, therefore, there are social, informal dimensions to the training programs that may be as important as the substantive material that is presented.

From the bank's perspective, the training programs create an environment that reinforces staff retention and growth. Employees begin to "speak the same language," use common acronyms, and, over time, take on a corporate identity and loyalty. The socialization process is important to the bank because it reinforces the employees' bonds to the company. Thus, when highly skilled bank personnel are wooed by other major multinational corporations, they are less likely to accept the offers. The bank, of course, has made a substantial investment in these employees that it does not wish to lose.

The Citicorp training program has been so successful and prominent in Jakarta that the bank is now offering many of its courses to nonbank employees, especially the employees of major clients. They have "sold" courses to multinationals such as United Tractor, as well as to many local firms in Indonesia and other Asian states. The net effect of these activities is twofold; first, Indonesian nationals who gain employment with the bank have at their disposal the resources to maintain professional competencies for their entire careers and have access to the personnel and materials that will keep them at the forefront of their disciplines; second, in broader terms, the activities demonstrate what has also been observed in the United States — that major banks and corporations attach great importance to continuing employee refreshment and are willing to take on a major training function not presently being carried out by institutions of higher learning. The lesson of this corporate policy is not lost on indigenous corporations.

The Citicorp/Indonesia Training Program illustrates several important points concerning continuing education in developing countries. First, training activities such as these contribute to the maintenance of international standards in several fields. They permit Indonesians to be continuously exposed to techniques, procedures, and substantive innovations that are at the frontiers of the banking profession. Second, they underscore the point that, with American corporate stimuli, Indonesians who have and have not studied abroad can gain a heightened awareness of the need to maintain skill levels as a lifelong learning process rather than as a once-in-a-lifetime formal educational experience. This awareness is a necessary step if Indonesia, over time, is to develop the indigenous capacity to compete at accepted international levels. Third, they illustrate how a combination of talents from Indonesia and from the United States can work synergistically so that the net benefit to Citicorp and the Indonesian work force is greater than the sum of their individual contributions.

2. Arthur Young Accounting Training Program

The training program at Arthur Young, one of America's "big eight" accounting firms, is notable in several respects. Arthur Young hires only graduates of Indonesian universities, a policy dictated by a government regulation that provides that only graduates of such universities are eligible to become certified public accountants (CPAs). Prospective employees are recruited on the basis of their personalities, English-language abilities, scores on accounting tests administered by Arthur Young, and interviews with senior management in the firm's comfortable offices in downtown Jakarta.

When employees first join Arthur Young, they are given an orientation seminar that reviews work ethics, office policies, the principles of Indonesian taxation, and the role of computers in accounting. Several of these seminars are taught in English, while others are in Indonesian.

A major feature of employment with Arthur Young is that accountants are programmed through step-by-step evaluations of their work in Jakarta. At various points in their careers, they are sent to regional training programs — sometimes in Indonesia, other times in Hong Kong, Singapore, and Malaysia. In each case the training sessions involve examinations and grading; the scores are among the measures used to evaluate employees for positions of greater responsibility within the firm. Each employee spends two weeks each year in such courses. A major thrust of the courses is to teach employees the appropriate "defensive posture" with which to protect the client's interests in the Indonesian system.

In some respects the training process can be viewed as a manifestation of "technology transfer," whereby American educational techniques and values are provided to Indonesian nationals. Thus, the American firm, in a very real sense, takes care of its own "aftercare," minimizing the prospects for decline of professional competencies. Indeed, at Arthur Young, virtually all the top-level personnel have served, at one time or another, as instructors in these training programs. "Learning by teaching" seems to be another important mechanism for maintaining competencies.

Arthur Young also offers an intensive three-week English language course for its non-American employees and operates a large educational center in Reston, Virginia, where a wide variety of subjects are offered to American and foreign employees. Arthur Young thus seriously competes with graduate-level programs in several fields. While many of its courses are intended solely for internal use, others, like those at Citicorp, are also designed for clients of the firm.

Senior managers at Arthur Young with whom we spoke noted that a few of the other Big Eight accounting firms have training programs of this type and scale, but that this is not the practice with Japanese or German firms. On balance, it was the view at Arthur Young that the principal challenge in these training programs is not to transmit the substantive material per se. Rather it is to cope effectively with cultural differences and to adapt accounting practices and techniques developed in the United States to an Indonesian society marked by a different pace of activity, customs, mores, and expectations, in addition to a very different tax structure.

Arthur Young has unequivocally discovered that maintenance of professional competencies cannot be divorced from the political culture in which the training takes place. It is neither feasible nor desirable to import wholesale cassette-type courses and training sessions developed with the assumptions and expectations found in the American workplace. Instead, if the training is to be a meaningful, functional experience for the trainee, it is essential to take account carefully and systematically of the norms and values that dominate the political and economic climate of the developing country.

Like the Citicorp training program, the Arthur Young program increases the awareness of the need for continuing education among Indonesians exposed to it and also permits them to maintain standards at the level required to compete effectively in the modern world economy.

3. Caltex Training Program/Indonesia

A third corporate program designed explicitly to maintain professional competencies in Indonesia is the set of training activities run by the Caltex Pacific Corporation. Caltex Pacific is jointly owned by the Chevron and Texaco oil companies and, at present, accounts for roughly one-half of Indonesian oil production (approximately 1.5 million barrels per day).

The firm was founded in 1952. Initially its sole activity was drilling for oil, but gradually the company began to need to teach welders and machinists how to confront the specialized tasks required in offshore oil exploration. Now, after more than three decades, training programs of all types account for 12 percent of the budget of this huge corporation.

At the lowest level of management, a supervisory development program has been implemented. It is designed to instruct employees in approaches to modern business management problems. These problems include how to motivate employees, how to improve interpersonal and organizational communication, and how to monitor attitudinal change. Supervisors are instructed in the importance of feedback through evaluation forms. At a higher level, Caltex offers a management development program for more senior employees in which a major emphasis is the promotion of cross-cultural relationships. Acknowledging the wide cultural differences within Indonesian society between Muslims and non-Muslims, Javanese and non-Javanese, and the like, the Caltex program educates managers in the norms and values of the various groups with whom they are most likely to come into contact. According to Caltex employees and others, this program is so special that the training programs are themselves a major incentive for Indonesians to join the company.

When Caltex employees have achieved certain levels of seniority or are in need of specialized training, they are sent to the United States at corporate expense to obtain master's degrees in their chosen fields of study from American graduate schools. It is stated corporate policy that the principal aim of this training is "Indonesianization" — that is, to permit Indonesian employees to function more effectively within their own society. A decidedly secondary objective is "internationalization" of the employee — that is, to sensitize the individual to the international business community. Caltex, quite rightly in our view, places performance in the domestic milieu ahead of international effectiveness.

As Caltex employees rise in the company, they are required to complete a series of training programs. Satisfactory completion of one training program is required for promotion, which in turn permits employees access to the next level of training. Indeed, the Employee Development Advisory Committee takes training experience directly into account when assessing employees for promotion. The training programs therefore serve as a "scouting device" for identifying especially promising employees.

Caltex stresses the value of education for the children of their employees as well. The company provides substantial financial incentives to encourage children to achieve academic excellence. One feature of this program is a scholastic award competition. The first-prize winner each year is provided with six years of education in Indonesian institutions of higher learning followed by four and one-half years of fully funded education in the United States. The second-prize winner receives support for the Indonesian portion of the first prize. The two top awards include transportation, room and board, tuition, a monthly stipend, and the expenses of parental visits and attendance at the graduation ceremonies. Ten consolation prizes provide cash awards that can be used toward the costs of higher education. In short, the commitment by Caltex to lifelong learning takes on a variety of forms and is demonstrated by the allocation of substantial corporate resources to the education of both employees and their offspring.

One peculiar feature of the Caltex system is that employees are obligated to retire at age 55. Many employees are left with ten, 15, or more years of productive employment ahead of them. Most employees, we gathered, easily find positions with other oil companies or corporations engaged in various businesses because of the regular updating they have undergone. In essence, they take the Caltex training with them and apply it in their new corporate settings. Consequently, whether intentional or not, there is a rippling effect of the Caltex training program that surely pays major dividends to the nation in terms of maintaining professional competencies.

4. IPB/Bogor

A noteworthy characteristic of many developing countries that must be taken into account in the appraisal of programs to maintain skill levels is the marked difference between the attitudes and resources prevalent in the national capital and the perspectives and far more limited resources found in other areas of the country. It would be highly misleading to claim that, for example, programs that work reasonably effectively in Jakarta can be easily replicated in other urban or rural sections of Indonesia. We are therefore particularly grateful to have found a strong program at the Institut Pertanian Bogor (IPB), a significant agricultural research and training institute in Bogor, a small city about 60 kilometers south of Jakarta.

IPB was founded 40 years ago and served as an agricultural unit of the Dutch government during Indonesia's colonial period. In the late 1950s, agricultural experts from the University of Wisconsin, funded by a series of grants from the U.S. Agency for International Development, became associated with the institute. The Wisconsin Agricultural Project, as it came to be called, had as one of its initial tasks the job of training IPB's senior soil scientists, which was carried out by personnel from both the University of Wisconsin and the Mid-Western University Consortium for International Activities (MUCIA), which conducts a variety of international agricultural programs in developing countries.

Over time the Wisconsin involvement has moved through three distinct phases. In the first phase, Wisconsin and MUCIA personnel were heavily involved in instructing IPB faculty and staff and in carrying out various "line" functions within the institute. In the second phase, begun after about eight years, emphasis shifted to planning, institution building, and staff development. In the current third phase, which has been marked by a significant diminution of non-Indonesian involvement, the principal efforts have been reduced to long-range planning, helping IPB staff establish objectives, implementing curriculum modification, selected staff upgrading, assisting departmental teaching programs, and academic planning associated with the development of a new campus.

Cooperation between Indonesia and the United States at IPB began with manpower development. Initial stress was on advanced applied sciences, such as plant breeding. Instruction then shifted to the basic sciences, especially physics and chemistry. The first Indonesian graduates quickly became absorbed in the administration of the institution. The current generation is focusing instead on research (e.g., the problem of photosynthesis and how it can influence enzymes and produce high-yield crops; the relationship between climatology and agricultural productivity).

Over the years the research activities of the institute have grown increasingly sophisticated. Present plans call for a new information center, initiation of energy studies, application of remote sensing devices, and a national satellite program that could be useful for agricultural planning. Moreover, IPB has grown to benefit from the ASEAN connection. Through division of labor, each member of ASEAN has taken on particular specializations; IPB faculty and staff have studied certain subjects in the various ASEAN countries, just as their neighbors have studied with them. The following areas of specialization are presently in effect: tropical biology in Indonesia; English language in Singapore; agriculture in the Philippines; general science in Malaysia; and tropical medicine in Thailand. Clearly, Indonesia's part in this international cooperative association has had major payoffs for IPB.

IPB currently holds both a grant from the U.S. Agency for International Development (AID) and a substantial loan from the World Bank. The grant is for technical assistance funded at $1.7 million over four years. The loan is to cover the cost of training programs, as well as to establish a library and environmental studies center. In a generous gesture, the University of Wisconsin has turned over $100,000 in overhead funds to the institute in the last several years.

One of IPB's main missions since its inception has been to provide graduate education to Indonesians. It now teaches roughly 20 percent of the nation's undergraduates in agriculture but 80 percent of its graduate students. Moreover, IPB anticipates a 7 to 8 percent annual increase in student intake over the next several years, pointing toward a student body of 20,000 by the year 2000. To operate at these enrollment levels, IPB will need to triple its staff and move to an annual staff appointment level of 200. The challenges of this coming period are certain to be at least as demanding as those of institution building in the past decade, when several American universities were instrumental.

It would be highly desirable for new international educational relationships appropriate for these changed conditions to be developed in the immediate future. One of the principal goals of these relationships should be to limit the decay of the IPB faculty and staff. A judgment that institutions such as IPB have reached the point of development when assistance should cease would be both wrong and potentially destructive. The task will be to assist IPB in sustaining its strength under the pressures it will surely experience. This task will differ from institution building but will be no less potentially rewarding to both parties in the long run.

In the particular experience of IPB, personnel from both the University of Wisconsin and the University of Kentucky played central roles in technical assistance. The primary emphasis of the Kentucky contribution was to aid in institution building, whereas the focus of the Wisconsin efforts was to be a catalyst for new research and training initiatives. What was once a hierarchical relationship between the American teachers and their Indonesian pupils was transformed into a truly equal partnership in some areas and relatively modest levels of consultation in others.

This example of institution building in the early years and consulting in the later years is still another model by which professionals in developing countries can learn to maintain their knowledge at the forefront of their respective disciplines. This model also reflects the effectiveness of modest investments, which can be achieved only after years of close cooperation and mutual trust. It seems that great continuing value may come from sustained U.S. commitments to successful bilateral relationships of this kind. The evolution in the form and intensity of the relationship that has already occurred is entirely appropriate, but relationships of this kind can contribute mightily to the prevention of decay across entire institutions, like IPB, and they should be sustained on this plateau for an indefinite period.

5. Center for Strategic and International Studies/Jakarta

Shortly after President Sukarno was deposed in 1965, several supporters of his successor, President Suharto, established a small group that was intended to advise the highest levels of government about the medium-range and long-range strategic problems facing Indonesia. Two decades later this group has been transformed into a full-fledged policy studies and research center with many features similar to those of its counterparts in the United States, Britain, and other developed countries. The Center for Strategic and International Studies (CSIS) in Jakarta may well be unique within the developing countries in terms of its resources and the level of sophistication of its analysis.

Remembering that Indonesia is governed by an authoritarian regime, as are the vast majority of developing countries, we know that an institution like CSIS cannot function without the support of and the constraints imposed by the government. Nonetheless, over two decades, CSIS has emerged not merely as some quiet advisory arm of the official apparatus but also as a major research center with an international reputation for its study of political-military and economic questions that affect Indonesia and, more generally, Southeast Asia.

CSIS is located in a substantial building in a pleasant section of Jakarta and is in the process of a considerable expansion of its library, computer, and research facilities. When completed, the physical plant will rank in space and resources among the best in the world for an institution of its kind.

CSIS has long been directed by Jusuf Wanandi, who was originally trained as an aeronautical engineer in Denmark. Wanandi has built a well-funded think tank that serves, but is quasi-independent from, the Indonesian ministries of defense and foreign affairs. The center conducts both policy-relevant and historical research. Policy analysts (roughly 50) are able to reach the natural conclusions of their research, but, as an institution, CSIS is restricted to criticizing the government and its policies in private.

The center has many of the characteristics of any modern research institution. It publishes a monthly journal, in Indonesian and English, that is devoted largely to research by members of its staff and deals overwhelmingly with strategic problems in Indonesia and the local environment. An occasional paper series numbers approximately six issues annually. CSIS has a well-equipped research library and several on-line computer systems.

The chairman of the board of CSIS is a former Indonesian minister of education, and several other board members have had extensive experience in government in both the defense and nondefense sectors. This provides the institute with access to the highest level of decision makers. It is not uncommon for senior government officials, and occasionally President Suharto himself, to attend special seminars with CSIS staff to discuss contemporary policy problems.

Over the years the center has moved heavily into policy studies relevant to the health of the Indonesian economy. A majority of the research staff is now concerned with issues such as the economic development of the Pacific Basin, financial flows among oil-producing states, and regional stability within Indonesia. Since it is to be expected in the Indonesian political environment that an institution such as CSIS will act in a quasi-intelligence advisory role, it is important to emphasize the large quantity and high quality of open research that is conducted by the CSIS staff.

A major mechanism that the center uses to maintain the professional competencies of its staff is study abroad. Several of the leading figures in the institute studied economics at the graduate level at the University of California at Berkeley. In fact, there is a Berkeley "mafia" at CSIS that has counterparts in several government ministries. Active contacts are maintained between these individuals and their former teachers. Moreover, as may be expected, CSIS has developed ties with the RAND Corporation in Santa Monica, California, after which it is to some degree patterned. (RAND is officially categorized as a Federal Contract Research Center, which means it does not have to enter competitive bidding processes to receive government support. It was originally the think tank for the U.S. Air Force and still does considerable classified work for it, but for more than 20 years it has also been engaged in unclassified policy analyses and research of all sorts on problems of health, transportation, foreign policy, computer science, physics, and other fields of scholarly inquiry.)

A few members of the CSIS research staff have spent time in residence at RAND, either as visiting scholars or as students enrolled in RAND's doctoral training program in policy analysis, the RAND Graduate Institute. In turn, members of RAND's staff have been visiting scholars in residence at CSIS, and a number of joint research seminars involving members of both institutions have been held over the last several years. The close reciprocal relationships that have developed between these counterpart institutions represent one important way in which the developed world can assist intellectuals and professionals in the developing world resist decay.

As the center has moved more deeply into economic analysis, it has evidently become something of a bridge or transmission belt between the government and the private sector. Its seminars bring together senior individuals from both sectors. Its research addresses problems of common interest. And the CSIS staff makes an effort to point out the synergisms that can develop through closer business-government connections.

Obviously, CSIS retains a privileged place in Indonesian society. It performs a trusted advisory role for government agencies (although it is viewed with suspicion by some government officials precisely because it is independent enough to challenge current policy directions). It has a well-funded research program and ample resources for travel and publications. There is every sense, when one enters the center, that this institution is using its capacities to stay very much at the forefront of its fields of study and is in fact contributing substantial knowledge to the worldwide scholarly community on subjects of its own professional expertise.

It would appear that special organizational circumstances, close personal connections, and a political leadership sympathetic to such research activities are necessary conditions for centers such as CSIS to thrive in the political and economic environments of most developing countries.

On balance, these five Indonesian cases illustrate the range of possibilities available to developing countries for attacking the problem of professional decay. It can be done through technical assistance by on-site specialists, as in the case of IPB/Bogor. It can be done in cooperation with major multinational corporations that place continuing education high on their list of corporate priorities, as is the case with Citicorp, Arthur Young, and Caltex. Or it can be done with constant interaction between Indonesian scholars and their American counterparts, both at home and in the United States, as demonstrated by the CSIS. Each mode of interaction can play an important role in maintaining professional skills among specialists from developing countries after they have returned from study abroad.

Turkey

Turkey is geographically and psychologically at the intersection of Europe, Asia, and the Middle East. Its GNP per capita of $1,370 in 1982 places it at the top of the "lower middle-income" countries, roughly equidistant in wealth from Mexico and Indonesia. A nation of somewhat more than 45 million, it is by far the least populous of the three countries we studied.

Two decades ago it was observed that "the only political ideology that enjoys universal respectability and commands wide allegiance among the educated class is Turkish nationalism as formulated by Kemal Ataturk."[10] Ataturk established the modern Turkish Republic in 1923 and ruled it with an iron hand until his death in 1938. His major reforms, secularizing the institutions of government and "westernizing" society, have survived his death, as well as many subsequent turbulent experiences. Ataturk successfully gave women the right to vote and the encouragement to take their rightful place in all walks of Turkish society, discouraged the wearing of the fez (supposedly by ordering the beheading of anyone with one on!), and sought more generally to break Islam's hold on the educational, governmental, and commercial institutions of the society.

A respected student of the Turkish polity put Ataturk's efforts in perspective in the following way:

> For many Turks, the great transformation which has taken place in their country is to be defined, not merely in terms of economy or society or government, but of civilization. The essential change attempted by the Turks in their Revolution was one of Westernization — another step in the westward march of the Turkish people that began 1,000 years ago, when they renounced China and turned to Islam. Now, renouncing a large part though not the whole of their Islamic heritage, they have turned to Europe, and made a sustained and determined effort to adopt and

[10]Dankwart A. Rustow, "The Modernity of Tradition," in *Political Culture and Political Development*, ed. Lucian Pye (Princeton: Princeton University Press, 1965), p. 162.

47

apply the European way of life in government, society, and culture. Opinions differ as to the measure of success achieved in this attempt; there can, however, be no doubt that in large and important areas of the public life of Turkey the Westernizing revolution is accomplished and irreversible.[11]

Today, as for many years past, Turkish society divides into roughly three groups:

The first, including the military, the bureaucracy, and the parliamentarians, represent, in one form or another, the continuing tradition of the Ottoman ruling class. The second group, including the communications elites (journalists, writers, poets), party politicians, and educators, tend to mediate between these ruling elites and the rest of society. The remaining group, including interest groups and other socioeconomic elites, still play only a limited role in politics.[12]

In the last 30 years, Turkey has had to confront enormous domestic and international problems. Having received economic and military assistance under the Truman Doctrine of 1947 and thus having avoided a postwar communist takeover, Turkey joined the North Atlantic Treaty Organization (NATO) in 1952 together with Greece, without in any way settling its centuries-old disputes with this western neighbor. The island of Cyprus had long been one source of dispute, and in 1974 Turkish forces invaded the island. One of the by-products of the invasion was a five-year American embargo on military and economic assistance. In the course of this period, for many reasons, widespread violence erupted throughout Turkish society, with mass and random killings an everyday occurrence on street corners and college campuses. In 1980, a military coup d'etat restored order to the country and, in the view of many Turks, rescued it from the brink of civil anarchy.

In educational terms, the Turkish Republic has come a long way, but it still has a long way to go. When the republic was founded, it was estimated that only about 10 percent of the population were literate. By the early 1970s, however, primary education was compulsory for all children between ages seven and 12. Although it is estimated that large numbers of children in provincial areas still do not attend school, the national literacy rate has risen dramatically to at least 55 percent of the population aged six and over.

Turkey boasts a number of outstanding institutions of higher education, including the Middle East Technical University and the University of the Bosphorous, which we visited in the course of our study, but in national comparative statistical terms, the level of Turkish higher education is disappointingly low. According to World Bank statistics, in 1981 only 5 percent of the population aged 20–24 were enrolled in courses of higher education. The figure had risen slightly from 3 percent in 1960. Thus, Turkey is in the bottom quarter of lower middle-income developing countries and between Mexico and Indonesia in terms of our study.

Turkey was singled out in the late 1960s as having "graduated" from the "developing" to the "developed" country class and became no longer eligible for economic assistance from the U.S. Agency for International Development. By the early 1970s, major grant programs of the Ford and Rockefeller Founda-

[11]Bernard Lewis, *The Emergence of Modern Turkey, Second Edition* (London: Oxford University Press, 1966), p. 486.
[12]Pye, *Political Culture*, p. 185.

tions had been terminated as well. Despite many economic and social indicators to the contrary, Turkey was cut off from assistance because some American analysts had decided that the country had "made it" economically and that there were many other more deserving cases to support among the poorer countries of the world.

A major consequence of these decisions was that the flow of Turkish students to the United States began to dry up. The United States had, for example, welcomed more than 19,000 Turkish military personnel for training between 1950 and 1975. From 1975 through 1979, there was a complete embargo on Turkish military personnel studying in the United States. Only recently has the number of Turkish military studying in the United States been built back up to modest levels.

The Turkish armed forces, which include one of the largest standing armies in Europe, are, in size and effectiveness, not only by-products of a long, proud military tradition, but also reflections of the Turkish geostrategic position, which is marked by the sharing of borders with Iran, Iraq, and Syria in the south and east; Greece in the west; and Bulgaria and the Soviet Union in the north. Although Turkey has profited economically from the four-year Iran-Iraq war by remaining politically neutral and selling to both sides, borders with neither country are considered "friendly." Ironically, among all the states contiguous to it, Turkey has in recent years maintained the most cordial relations with Bulgaria, a member of the Warsaw Treaty Organization and a close ally of the Soviet Union. But this relationship has taken a sharp downturn since the Turkish-Bulgarian connections in the attempted assassination of the Pope were revealed and because reprisals were taken by the Bulgarian government against the substantial Turkish minority who live in Bulgaria. Management of the rivalry with Greece, perennial concern about Soviet intentions, and an endemic problem with Armenians who carry out acts of violence abroad in order to bring world attention to their grievance against the Turks (for actions taken by Turkish soldiers against Armenian civilians in 1915) are other very high foreign policy priorities for the government in Ankara. Historically, a consequence of Turkey's demanding geostrategic situation has been that the armed forces have been highly trained and have maintained close contact with the U.S. military, whereas most other key elements of Turkish society have been far more isolated from their counterparts in the international community and thus more prone to problems of intellectual and professional decay.

In economic terms, the Turkish government of Prime Minister Ozal, himself a professional economist, has in the last few years made the bold decision to open the economy to foreign investment and to reorient Turkish industry to an export strategy. Some political restrictions have been lifted, and it is widely assumed that a return to democratic processes will be intimately connected to progress on the economic front. A detailed analysis by *The Economist* observed:

> In the four years since the armed forces suppressed Turkey's terrorist slaughter, the country has been groping to find an economic and political formula that will bring it peace and prosperity. For the moment it has two novelties: a one-armed democracy and an open-armed economy. Neither is satisfactory, both are still changing — but change in Turkey is never as fast as its friends would wish. . . . If

his [Ozal's] economic policy is not a success, the prospects of a future for Turkey as a prosperous democracy are bleak.[13]

One of the by-products of this shift in policy has been a sharp rise in demand for professional manpower of a quality adequate for competition on the world stage.

An additional by-product of the political and economic situation is the effect on the Turkish academic community of the policies of Yok, the Turkish Council of Higher Education, which was established in 1981 to reform the system of colleges and universities in the country.[14] The government, responding to the anarchy that marked college campuses before it seized power, has sought to centralize decision-making authority in the hands of this body, which is governed by a council composed of eight professors elected by an interuniversity board, eight professors selected by the head of state, eight high-ranking civil servants selected by the council of ministers, and one member selected by the general staff.[15] In seeking to achieve uniform standards and to open up the doors of higher education to virtually all Turkish citizens who seek to pass through them, the council has adopted noble objectives. However, a negative consequence of these actions has been the flooding of Turkish universities with students who cannot be adequately handled by the faculty (it is commonplace to meet Turkish faculty who teach four courses each semester with several hundred students each without the benefit of any graduate assistants to help in grading). Moreover, faculty have lost their autonomy in many spheres of university operations, even in the number and type of examinations they may administer. With salaries at very low levels (the equivalent of $350 per month for a senior professor), many faculty are demoralized; a number are leaving universities for the private sector or for lucrative teaching appointments in Jordan, Libya, Saudi Arabia, or the Persian Gulf states that promise salary increases in excess of tenfold.

As a result of these circumstances, we found few cases of organized Turkish efforts to maintain skill levels at world-class standards. There are, we were told, simply too many far more pressing problems to worry about. Nonetheless, a few interesting cases presented themselves.

Turkish Cases

1. Yasar Holding/Izmir

Yasar Holding is one of the three largest Turkish-owned conglomerates in the country. With 35 manufacturing and trading companies, two foundations, and several representatives abroad, Yasar Holding is one of the most powerful, dynamic private enterprises in Turkey. The company provided Turkey with its first paint factory, its first private brewery, and its first sterilized milk and dairy products plant. Today it employs 6,600 people and has more than 16,000 shareholders.

---

[13]"Inshallah: A Survey of Turkey" in *The Economist* (November 3, 1984), pp. 5–20. (For a detailed account of Turkish economic strategy, see "Turkey: A Special Report" in *International Herald Tribune* (June 8-9, 1985).)
[14]The rationale for the establishment of Yok is provided in Ihsan Dogramaci, "The New Turkish Higher Education Law and Autonomy", a paper presented at the International Symposium on University Government and Autonomy (Ankara, Turkey: December 1981).
[15]"The Higher Education in Turkey: Results After Three Years" (mimeo) (Ankara, Turkey: June 1985).

Yasar Holding provides several educational and cultural services to its employees. A company-directed foundation provides scholarships for successful and talented children of limited means that enable them to continue and complete their studies at institutions in Turkey and abroad without financial problems. Another objective is to assist and accelerate the rapid growth of educational institutions throughout the country. In fact, Yasar Holding is taking a leading role in establishing a new, private university in Izmir that will specialize in management and computer science.

Yasar Holding has a very active employee-training program directed by a dynamic Turkish economist who was trained at the University of Chicago. This individual, recognizing the need for practical training programs for the corporation's staff, developed an in-house seminar program modeled along the lines of the Kraft Foods Management Development Seminars held in Chicago. Because of corporate connections between Yasar Holding's food divisions and the Kraft Food Company, Kraft made available the manuals and teaching materials used in its seminars. These materials were in turn translated into Turkish and modified to fit accepted practices in Turkish management and industrial settings. This program seems to be an admirable, and unquestionable, example of technological transfer.

At present programs have been established for general and middle managers throughout the company. (Clients of Yasar Holding are currently not eligible to attend these courses, but this policy may change shortly.) Because of the shortage of highly skilled personnel, Yasar executives say it is very difficult to send employees overseas for long periods (normally never in excess of six months). Consequently, the seminars provide a convenient mechanism for maintaining the skill levels of the company's employees while keeping them in the country.

Like a number of the corporate cases in Indonesia, Yasar Holding has begun to find that these courses, seminars, and training sessions are useful for identifying especially talented individuals worthy of rapid promotion.

2. Mobile Training Teams/Ankara

During our stay in Turkey, we had fruitful discussions with Americans and Turkish nationals involved with the International Military Education and Training Program (IMET), which grants American assistance for Turkish training, and the Joint U.S. Military Mission for Aid to Turkey (JUSMAT). In the course of these discussions, we came across a method of instruction that we believe to have potential for wider applicability in the civilian sector. Termed "Mobile Training Teams," the approach involves sending several (usually two to five) specialists in a particular field from the United States to Turkey to spend a few weeks in intensive interaction with Turkish nationals in need of instruction in their fields of specialization. For example, a Mobile Training Team under JUSMAT generally includes two U.S. English-language experts who visit several Turkish schools to train English-language instructors in new foreign-language teaching techniques. Or, as an additional example, the U.S. Army has sent teams of five specialists in ballistic welding to Turkey to teach Turkish maintenance personnel newly developed methods for repairing damaged tanks.

We believe this kind of concentrated effort may profitably be applied to a wide variety of other fields that are relevant to developing countries — from crop protection to the application of computer techniques in commercial banking. We sought opinions about this approach from Turkish nationals in the private sector, in academia, and in government agencies. The overwhelming response was positive. What was required, they said, was a coordinated effort in which the needs of constituencies within developing countries were carefully identified and matched with the capabilities and specializations of experts brought from the United States. Intensive short courses could be manageable, in terms of time constraints, on both sides, and the net effect would be the maintenance of professional and intellectual skills at the most advanced levels.

3. Labor/Management Relations/Istanbul

In the faculty of economics at Istanbul University, an interesting program funded by the AFL/CIO Institute in Washington, D.C., and USAID is in operation. The institute has established an Asian-American Free Labor Institute (AFLI) to which Turkish specialists in labor relations may belong.

AFLI has an office in Ankara and funds programs in trade-union education and research. AFLI provides technical expertise, equipment, and financial support to 30 Turkish trade unions and enlists American and Turkish scholars as part of its activities. For example, shop stewards in Turkish factories are trained in labor law that concerns the rights and freedoms of Turkish workers. AFLI personnel, based in Turkey, together with faculty members from Istanbul's faculty of economics, prepare the necessary training programs and materials, adapting techniques and concepts supplied by AFLI in Washington to the special circumstances of the Turkish work environment. Not only is this experience valuable for the Turkish shop steward, but it also provides a fine opportunity for the Turkish scholar to become conversant in the latest approaches of the AFL/CIO and their relevance to the Turkish situation.

Turkish scholars with whom we spoke claimed that these experiences were invaluable in sharpening their skills as mediators in labor-management disputes. As university-based personnel, these faculty are frequently invited by the government, corporations, and labor unions to serve as mediators in a wide variety of contexts. Through AFLI, among other sources, they remain up-to-date on the current literature and practices in their field and are able to introduce these concepts into the classroom and to apply them in real-world situations.

These three cases illustrate that, even under difficult economic and political conditions, Turkish institutions have maintained an awareness of the need to maintain skill levels and have adopted a variety of measures to address that need. The Yasar Holding case suggests that continuing education programs can be adopted with relatively little difficulty in Turkish corporations to keep personnel who received their education either at home or in the United States at the frontiers of their respective fields of specialization. The AFLI case signifies an effective means of promoting Turkish-American interaction to the direct benefit of Turkish scholars who have studied previously in American institutions of higher education. And the Mobile Training Teams suggest a promising mode of future interaction between American specialists and Turkish institutions that has already proved its effectiveness in bilateral military cooperation.

The United States

American Cases

The retardation of intellectual and professional decay in developing countries is, of course, not limited to indigenous programs in particular Third World states. A number of major efforts based in the United States, but involving personnel from the developing world, also play a useful role in retraining and renewal. In order to gain some sense of the diversity of these programs, we seek to describe, in summary fashion, five such efforts, which we believe illustrate the range of activities that are presently available and worthy of continued support.

1. The Hubert H. Humphrey North-South Fellowship Program

The Hubert H. Humphrey North-South Fellowship Program provides one-year fellowships in the United States for midcareer professionals from developing countries. The program was begun in 1978 as a tribute to former Vice President Humphrey and his commitment to Third World development. It has been funded since its inception by the U.S. Information Agency (USIA) as a Fulbright Mutual Exchange activity and is administered by the Institute of International Education (IIE).

The central purpose of the Humphrey Fellowship Program is to provide Fellows with precisely the sort of refresher training and career development opportunities that are the subject of this study. Fellows are based at universities within departments that have demonstrated strengths in subject areas of direct interest to the Fellows and that have experience in administering development programs abroad. Individually tailored programs, including academic courses, independent study, training, and internships, are planned for each Fellow by specially appointed university coordinators and advisers. The Fellows are, for the most part, professional public-sector managers whose fields of specialization are normally drawn from agriculture, health and nutrition, public administration, planning, or resource management.

The program has grown in scope and magnitude each year. In 1984–85, for example, there were 151 Fellows from 73 developing countries. This represented an increase in the number of Fellows of 14 percent from 1983–84, as well as an increase in the number of countries participating. The program began with a pilot group of 27 Fellows from 24 countries and has grown steadily to its current level. The 1984–85 group was made up of midcareer professionals averaging 36 years of age; about 50 percent of the Fellows held either master's or doctoral degrees. It is estimated that a similar number (150) will be awarded fellowships for the 1986–87 academic year. Approximately 15 universities across the United States serve as host institutions for the Fellows each year.

Participation among African and Latin American countries has risen throughout the life of the program. This increased participation is in accordance with the policy of the Board of Foreign Scholarships, which directs that one Humphrey Fellowship be reserved for each country submitting a qualified candidate. The policy serves to encourage small and newly founded countries to submit applications. In 1983–84, countries participating for the first time included Algeria, Guinea Bissau, Lesotho, Madagascar, Somalia, Swaziland, and Zimbabwe.

The selection of Fellows involves nomination by the government of the developing country, screening of applications by the local USIA post, and then final determination and placement by the IIE Humphrey Fellowship staff in New York and the program coordinators at the individual universities around the country.

The fellowships are one-year, nondegree grants that stress both academic course work and exposure to administrative practice. During their initial stay on campus, the Fellows are urged to draft a plan of action for their year in the United States. This plan includes provision for academic courses in areas of interest to the Fellows. Stress is placed on appropriate professional development activities on and off campus. Thus, Fellows are provided with a first-rate opportunity to update their knowledge in their respective professional fields, away from the demands of their daily routine back home. Fellows also identify those organizations in the immediate area of their universities and throughout the United States that they wish to visit. The organizations may be U.S. government offices in Washington, state or local offices, corporations, nonprofit institutions, or multinational organizations such as the World Bank and the United Nations. Fellows are encouraged to become familiar with professional associations and attend their annual conferences. Of particular importance is that aspect of the program in which Fellows seek out organizations with which they can have professional affiliations (i.e., structured assignments lasting from ten to 60 days). This experience provides the Fellows with invaluable exposure to the substantive issues and work environment of institutions where work is being done at the forefront of their professional fields.

The broad range of academic and professional development activities is enhanced by special seminars for the Humphrey Fellows that are arranged at each university. The seminars deal with subjects of specific interest to the Fellows and often involve presentations by them regarding administrative situations and development problems faced in their own countries. Overall, the program seeks to expand the Fellows' experience in working with the international community of professionals who deal regularly with matters of economic development. It is through study, experience, and exposure to such professionals that the leadership abilities of the Humphrey Fellows are enhanced.

It should be emphasized that an important intangible dimension to the program is the experience Fellows gain in close, continuous interaction with their peers in the university setting. When eight to 12 midcareer officials from governments throughout the developing world are in constant contact over a ten-month period, the sharing of experiences and perspectives provides each Fellow with valuable insights that are an important means for professional growth and renewal.

In our judgment this combination of intellectual, professional, and social interaction over a sustained period is a highly effective means of combating the decay and demoralization that often strike midcareer public-sector officials in the developing, as well as the developed, world.

2. The Harvard University Center for International Affairs Fellows Program

The Center for International Affairs (CFIA) is a multidisciplinary research institution within Harvard University. Founded in 1958, the center seeks to provide a stimulating environment for a diverse group of scholars and practitioners studying various aspects of international affairs. Its purpose is the development and dissemination of knowledge concerning the basic subjects and problems of international relations through the application of interdisciplinary social science research. Major center research programs include national security affairs; U.S. relations with Europe, Canada, and Japan; African studies; Middle Eastern studies; Latin American and Iberian studies; nonviolent sanctions in conflict and defense; and international economic policy. At any given time, over 160 individuals are working at the center, including faculty members from Harvard and neighboring institutions, practitioners of international affairs, visiting scholars, research associates, postdoctoral fellows, and graduate and undergraduate student associates.

When the CFIA was established in 1958 under the leadership of four Harvard faculty members — Robert Bowie from law, Henry Kissinger from political science, and Edward Mason and Thomas Schelling from economics — the mission of the center was captured in these words from the first annual report: "Our capacity to achieve the promise and avoid the perils of the modern age depends first, on deeper knowledge of the forces making for change, and second, on increased understanding of the impact of these forces in the international order. The required studies can seldom be done by government or officials immersed in pressing current activities. The Center for International Affairs was founded in the belief that Harvard has unusual resources for basic research of this kind."

In 1960 the CFIA recruited Benjamin Brown, a Columbia-trained historian then affiliated with the American University in Beirut, to direct the Fellows program. Under his leadership, an initial group of one dozen Fellows — practitioners from different countries drawn from the diplomatic service, the civil service, and the military — came to the center for an academic year of advanced study and research. These Fellows brought their practical experience to the research conducted at the university and used the facilities of the university for their professional and personal growth.

The agenda of the CFIA expanded greatly from the early 1960s to the 1980s, from initial concentration on European and security issues to concern with many of the key problems affecting economic and political development in Asia, Africa, and Latin America. The Fellows program grew from 12 to 25 during this period, and their geographical base became far more diversified than in the early years of the program.

Like the Humphrey Fellows, the CFIA Fellows are not degree candidates. They normally audit courses offered at Harvard, MIT, the Fletcher School of Law and Diplomacy of Tufts University, and other neighboring academic institutions. In addition they attend weekly luncheon seminars to compare experiences. These seminars supplement the very rich seminar series at CFIA and in other parts of Harvard on a wide range of issues in international affairs. In addition, each Fellow is expected to write a major research paper of 60 to 100 pages on a subject directly related to his professional field of specialization. Several of the papers have been published in the CFIA's occasional paper series, and a few have been expanded and published as books.

Funds are provided by the sponsoring government to cover the costs of each Fellow's residence at the center. The quality, promise, and stature of the Fellows over the years has been exceedingly high. Since the center has always focused not only on basic research in the fundamental problems of international affairs but also on their implications for public policy, a truly synergistic relationship has developed between the practical perspectives of the Fellows and the scholarly ambience of the university community.

Like the Humphrey Fellows, the CFIA Fellows take several trips during the academic year to become better acquainted with the wide range of institutions in the United States concerned with their fields of specialization. The academic stimulation, peer interaction, participation in the socialization processes of the Cambridge community, selected travel, and writing of major research papers combine to permit the Fellows to acquire state-of-the-art knowledge of their chosen fields. Moreover, an active alumni association ensures that the Fellows remain in contact with each other so that they can continue to share experiences and perspectives long after they have returned to their home countries.

The Harvard CFIA Fellows Program remains a small, elite activity. But its components, in our judgment, should serve as a useful model for other research centers in the United States, as well as in the developing world.

3. The American Studies Program of the American Council of Learned Societies (ACLS)

The American Studies Program, begun in the 1950s with assistance from the Ford Foundation, has continued to date with Ford support, in addition to support from many other public and private sponsors in the United States and the countries where it operates. It is in many respects the paragon of programs to resist decay. During its early years, this program set out to create strong communities of "Americanists" in Europe (West and East), parts of Asia, and Australia by the establishment of chairs, libraries, and research and teaching centers. Many of these early efforts "took" and vibrant American Studies communities came into being, in some cases with their own societies, networks, and other elements of scholarly infrastructure. The cores of these communities contained mainly specialists in the humanities and social sciences (especially history, literature, sociology, and political science), but American Studies soon also included members of the professions (including law, education, and architecture).

For most of the last two decades, the ACLS program has concentrated on nourishing and sustaining the communities that were created during this early period by providing fellowships to allow both promising and prominent Americanists to refresh themselves in the American material. The primary target group has consisted of younger scholars, usually but not always in academic posts, on the average less than a decade into their careers. Fellows are provided with a year (renewable for a second year in a few cases) at an American university to conduct research, audit courses and seminars, and to participate in the intellectual life of the institution. In practically all cases, the Fellows have studied in the United States prior to their ACLS fellowship, many to obtain their doctorates. The relationship between the refreshment they receive at a time of greater maturity and their original doctoral study may be compared to the relationship between a booster shot and a vaccination. The relatively few senior short-term, several-month visits provided by the ACLS are like second booster shots for a select few who play key leadership roles in their home communities.

The success of this remarkable program seems attributable to at least two factors. First, the program was operated from its inception to 1985 with extraordinary sensitivity and efficiency by a single director, Richard Downer. Second, it became a truly cooperative effort between the United States and the countries that it served. After 1970, sponsorship was shared by a variety of funding sources, which came from both ends of the cooperative effort. At the operational level, the selection process was also joint, with prescreening being conducted, whenever practicable, in the countries of origin and final selections being made by a committee of American academics.

Three features crucial to the success of the ACLS program are, first, carefully conducted interviews by the director with all candidates in the home countries; second, the award of fellowships strictly on merit; and third, the serious attention paid to the selection of the best possible locations for Fellows to spend their time (normally universities, libraries, archives, or research institutes). Over time, the director and the U.S. selection committee have gained much experience and sophistication in appraising references and judging the reception candidates will receive from an American host. Over the years, the nearly universal high quality of the Fellows has eased the task of recruiting and placing excellent applicants. The prestige of the program has made receipt of a fellowship or of a Fellow a prize rather than a responsibility. Alumni of the program, most of whom have remained in American Studies during their careers, now number among the most distinguished citizens of those countries served.

American Studies is an exceptional, or at least an extreme, subject area for our purposes. Those who pursue it in other countries cannot avoid decay without periodic visits to the United States. All the same, the challenge of American Studies and the successful response to the ACLS Program do demonstrate what can be accomplished by a carefully crafted decay-prevention effort. In part as a consequence of the hope and sustenance provided to hundreds of scholars around the world by the ACLS, American Studies has remained strikingly vigorous in other countries, often in contrast to fields in which decay seems to spread far more quickly. American benefits from this vigor have been insightful exposure to perspectives on American culture and problems by persons with a strikingly different experience and opportunities for cooperative research on topics, such as migration, to which joint endeavor is essential.

4. The Scientists and Engineers in Economic Development Program (SEED) of the National Science Foundation (NSF)*

The NSF is the principal federal agency responsible for advancing and promoting science in the United States. Because science knows no national borders, NSF is authorized to engage in international cooperative activities. To this end, a division of international programs exists to help meet the needs of scientists for international interchange and to assist in the development and implementation of scientific activities and programs that support U.S. foreign policy objectives.

In connection with this latter mission, the SEED program was established by NSF in 1971 and funded by the U.S. Agency for International Development. It had three objectives: to test the effectiveness of individual U.S. university scientists and engineers working with foreign counterparts in developing countries on projects that contributed to economic development; to stimulate more effective coupling of developing-country research and educational institutions with development priorities; and to establish long-term collaborative relationships between U.S. and foreign scientific institutions. This statement of goals is not precisely what would be expected of a project designed to resist intellectual and professional decay in developing countries, but it is certainly close. Between 1972 and 1979, when the program ended, 191 grants, totalling approximately $1.7 million, were awarded under SEED for work in more than 50 countries. In the 1980s, the SEED program's purpose continues to be reflected in an attenuated Science in Developing Countries Program (SDC) that permits small grants, not in excess of $20,000, by NSF for similar purposes.

Most international scientific cooperation has, as a by-product of its main objective, scientific advancement, some positive impact on the intellectual and professional vigor of both scientific communities involved. What was distinctive about SEED was that this by-product became the main objective. In this respect it may be unique in American experience. An excellent evaluation of the SEED experience, which uses conventional projects of international scientific cooperation as a comparison group, illuminates the results of the program. A survey of all participants in SEED projects and a selection of others, with an extremely high response rate, yielded the data for the evaluation. It is possible to note only some of the most relevant highlights here.

It is clear that the SEED and comparison scientists clearly recognized the different nature of their assignments and established distinct goals and priorities. When asked to identify "objectives for participating in activity," most of the SEED scientists (74.5 percent) picked "to disseminate knowledge to a foreign science community through teaching or lecturing" and (72.6 percent) "to plan, establish, or strengthen relationships between U.S. and foreign scientific institutions." Comparison group scientists, on the other hand, picked (82.9 percent) "to collect data specimens essential to my research" and (68.6 percent) "to stimulate my research in new or different directions."

One consequence of the distinct objectives of the SEED program was that

*The information and quotations given here about SEED come from the "Evaluative Study of the Scientists and Engineers in Economic Development (SEED) Program, Final Report: Participant Survey," prepared by Koray Tanfer and Lee Robeson for the Division of International Programs, National Science Foundation, Washington, D.C., March 1982.

SEED participants engaged in activities different from those of the comparison group. It is best to quote the evaluation on this point.

Nearly one-half (45%) of the SEED members were involved in teaching one or more courses, as compared to only ten percent of COMPARISON members. Similarly, almost nine in ten SEED, but four in ten COMPARISON, members were engaged in activities geared to improving the research and/or teaching capabilities of a foreign science institution. Both SEED (69%) and COMPARISON (51%) groups were involved in collaborative research; however, 82 percent of the COMPARISON, as opposed to 59 percent of the SEED, group members said that the research activity was a continuation of research conducted at home (in the US). . . . Eighty-four percent of the SEED group was involved in efforts to link host scientific capabilities to the socioeconomic goals of the country, while only 46 percent of the COMPARISON group was involved in such an effort. It is not surprising, therefore, that the COMPARISON group spent 59 percent of its time in field work, gathering data or specimens. The SEED group, on the other hand, spent 25 percent and 14 percent of its time, on the average, lecturing and discussing research, and teaching courses, respectively; in contrast, the COMPARISON group spent nine percent and two percent in lecturing/discussing research and teaching, respectively. In other words, while more than one-third of the time SEED scientists spent abroad was devoted to teaching and lecturing, COMPARISON scientists spent only one-tenth of the time in the same activities. Moreover, the average amount of time spent teaching a course was nearly twice as long for the SEED group (15 weeks) as for the COMPARISON group (nine weeks).

The evaluators summarize this difference in activity very nicely.

The most significant differences between the two groups lie in the activities undertaken, and the stated objectives. SEED activity is primarily geared to collaborative work, with a view to increasing the capabilities of scientific and technical institutions in developing countries. The COMPARISON group seems to be more intent upon pursuing their own research interests, and the activities undertaken center around this main goal. Hence, despite the fact that both groups are composed of scientists with approximately similar backgrounds, there are distinct differences in their purposes and consequently in the scope of their activities.

The perception by the two groups of obstacles to attainment of their different objectives illuminates the general issues discussed above.

The three most important problems, ranked as such by the respondents, are perhaps indicative of the activities in which the groups engaged. The low quality of both scientific work and resources was mentioned by both groups. SEED members, however, also indicated the inadequate cooperation and assistance of the foreign government agency to be an important problem. Scientists in the COMPARISON group mentioned the difficulties in obtaining licenses or approval of specimens and equipment.

The evaluation of SEED attempts to discover not only objective but also subjective outcomes of the program, as compared to conventional cooperative international scientific research. Obviously these subjective outcomes were related to the objectives, and here the differences were marked.

While SEED scientists considered foreign results as important outcomes of their activity, COMPARISON members were more concerned with US results exclusively related to their own research, professional advancement, or improvements in their institution's capability. For instance, nearly twice as many SEED (51.6%) as COMPARISON scientists (30.0%) mentioned the improvement of the research capability of a foreign science institution. Similarly, 54 percent of SEED, but only eight percent of COMPARISON, scientists considered improvement of the curriculum of a foreign science institution as an important positive result. Almost three times as many SEED as COMPARISON scientists (47.8% vs 18.4%, respectively) mentioned as an important positive outcome an increase in the relevance of the scientific research in the foreign country to the country's social or economic goals.

The bipolarization of the outcomes, as measured by the positive results mentioned, becomes more apparent when we look at the importance attached to the results. Respondents were asked to indicate the three most important results. Improvement of foreign research capability was the most frequently mentioned outcome among the top three cited by SEED scientists. In contrast, this outcome was not among the three most important cited by the COMPARISON group; instead, the most frequently mentioned outcome among the top three was advancement of their own research, resulting in publications or other written products.

With these differing objectives taken into account, the SEED program was judged by its participants to be highly successful.

More than one-half of the SEED scientists indicated that "to improve the curriculum of courses offered by a foreign science institution" was an important objective; of these scientists, approximately 86 percent indicated that this was a positive result of their activity. Similarly, approximately six of ten SEED scientists cited "improving the relevance of the scientific research in a foreign country to its economic or social goals" and "improving the research capabilities of a foreign science institution" among their most important objectives. It appears that about 60 percent of these scientists realized their expectations.

Similarly, 63 percent of the COMPARISON scientists aimed to stimulate their research, and it seems that a great majority of them met their expectations. For the COMPARISON group, the one-to-one correspondence of objectives and results is not as obvious as in the case of SEED scientists; however, their expectations about data and specimen collection, information acquisition, and advancement of own research seem to have been met.

Predictably, more than twice the number of SEED scientists (38.5 percent) discerned negative personal outcomes from their participation in international projects than did COMPARISON scientists (16.4 percent).

The following were the three most important negative results for SEED scientists:
• Loss of time at home, which set the scientist back in his/her research
• Absence disruptive to training of graduate students
• Activity abroad did not contribute to the possibility of promotion at home

The COMPARISON scientists also indicated that "disruptiveness to training graduate students" and "loss of time in research at home" were important negative results.

The experience of the pioneering SEED Program, as revealed in this evaluation, suggests several things. First, cooperative scientific programs designed to assist the scholarly communities of the developing world can be operated successfully. Second, the outcomes that they yield are almost certainly not acquired automatically as a by-product of conventional international scientific cooperation. Third, there is much to be gained from the experience of programs like SEED for future planning.

5. Fulbright Scholar Program

The Fulbright Program, which is administered by the Council for International Exchange of Scholars (CIES) in Washington, has probably done more than any other program anywhere at any time to retard the process of decay of competencies in Third World countries. It has arranged for the exchange of scholars between the United States and most other countries of the world on a massive scale. In 1984–85, more than 800 scholars moved in each direction. The preponderance of American scholars abroad (529 of 805) served as lecturers, while a larger proportion of visiting scholars in the United States (649 of 817) came as researchers. Undoubtedly most Fulbright exchanges help to sustain the intellectual communities of the cooperating countries just as they enrich the American institutions that send faculty abroad and serve as hosts. Moreover, all indications are that the Fulbright competitions are administered with rigorous fairness. The program has been increasingly decentralized over the years, with both joint funding and joint decision making administered by binational Fulbright commissions. There is no evidence of any tendency to move beyond strict scholarly criteria.

Recently the Fulbright Program has experimented with new modes of exchange, which include "groups or teams of grantees working in a collaborative setting." One recent example is the participation of four American economists and a political scientist in a regional research project on inflation stabilization in Argentina, Brazil, Chile, Ecuador, and Peru. Another recent innovation is to embed visiting scholars more firmly in American institutions as "scholars-in-residence." Still another new approach, for which we heard universal praise during our visit to Turkey and which responds directly to the problem of decay, is to provide funds to American grantees to purchase needed books and teaching materials related to their country for their host institutions. This is now permitted in Eastern Europe, the Soviet Union, and Turkey, but it can, and in our view should, be extended throughout.

A major obstacle to recruitment by the Fulbright Program of exceptionally distinguished participants in both directions of the exchange — the kinds of people who are likely to be more effective in the prevention of decay — is the constraint imposed on levels of stipend and minimum periods of stay. However, there is strong evidence that this problem is appreciated and that action will be taken to correct it. In his annual report for 1984, the chairman of the CIES, Stanley Katz, wrote: "This seems to be the point at which we ought to create more flexible grants. Shorter periods of time, higher stipends, more grants for research would all increase the appeal of Fulbright for some scholars. The innovative grants and projects launched by many of the Fulbright commissions in the past year already have gone a long way to increase the range and quality of participants in the program."

It appears that the Fulbright Program has gradually moved away from its initial straightforward concentration on the support of individuals in the conduct of teaching and research. Indirectly, the program has addressed and contributed to the solution of the decay problem all along. If the program is to do more in this direction, however, it will be necessary to accept that communities of scholars, which are, in part at least, more complex than simply the sum of individuals who make them up, are a proper subject of concern. If the Fulbright Program accepts this larger perspective and more extensive charge, the opportunities for improvement of the conditions of decay are very great indeed. It would be neither desirable nor necessary for the Fulbright Program to change fundamentally either its method of operation or many of its program decisions in order to be useful in this regard. It would be necessary to make some course corrections in the level and quality of certain participants, in the kinds of teaching and research to be encouraged, and in the types of activity to be monitored in the countries it serves. Measures of success, moreover, would be adjusted from the relatively simple, quantifiable magnitudes of books and articles published and courses taught to the health of intellectual and professional communities. The problem of measurement may be greatly increased, but the contribution to international education will be increased even more.

VII.
Prevention
of Decay:
Policies and
Practices

Increased resistance to and reversal of intellectual and professional decay can be obtained in a wide variety of ways. In this section we describe and comment on a range of alternative policies and practices that, in the main, were suggested to us by a large number of persons in the countries we visited. Some of the devices must be implemented by the domestic authorities in the countries where the problem exists. Other devices, however, are program possibilities for friendly First World countries that wish to be helpful. Some actions are of wide-ranging global character. Others are quite small and precise. We believe that they all deserve careful scrutiny. They are presented here in the form of simple injunctions.

Policies and Practices for the Third World

1. Information and advice. Acquaint students fully and frankly, before they depart for study abroad, with what educational opportunities are available overseas and what demands will be made of them upon their return home. A sophisticated appreciation of national need may be inculcated quite effectively by insisting, where possible, on relevant work experience prior to overseas study and on students' systematic predeparture examination of their own history and society. This practice may forestall disappointment with the value of the education acquired and will ensure that the education will be put to work in a useful, and therefore satisfying, fashion upon return home. We came to appreciate intensely the value of the sophisticated international educational-advisory services provided by the USIS, Fulbright commissions, and various private bodies in the countries we visited.

2. *Payment of competitive rates of return.* Compensate graduates of foreign study adequately and uninterruptedly in amounts approaching long-term market levels so that they will not be drawn away from the tasks for which they were trained. Remember that for many students trained abroad relevant market criteria are necessarily global. Even a brief interlude during which compensation is seriously below market levels may be enough to bring about a permanent exodus from a field where human capital was built up at great personal and social expense. We witnessed a migration of experienced technical scholars from Turkey to oil-rich Arab countries in the Middle East after their real incomes were reduced relative to others in the economy on grounds of distributive justice.

The common practice in developing countries of having professionals and intellectuals hold multiple jobs in order to cope with low salaries seems to be an especially strong enemy of continued high-level accomplishment. We are aware that payment of world-scale salaries to some persons in poverty-stricken developing countries seems both utopian and unfair. But just as growth and successful economic competition on the world stage often require use of and payment for complex, expensive physical capital, so also is effective participation in worldwide intellectual circles contingent on use of and payment for equally valuable human capital.

3. *Rewards for accomplishment.* Reward intellectuals and professionals, in terms of both personal compensation and honor, according to merit that is determined as much as possible by peer review. Nothing destroys morale and incentives to remain up-to-date more quickly than a reward system based on social position, personal loyalty, political respectability, and other criteria unrelated to the performance being judged. We do, however, realize the practical difficulty of implementing this recommendation in developing countries gripped by authoritarian traditions.

We perceived what seemed to be inadequate appreciation of the value of nonmonetary components of aggregate compensation to intellectuals and professionals, in particular the value of independence, freedom, command of their craft, and personal dignity. In Turkey, a recent university reform removed much of the autonomy from universities and, seemingly, much of the status from the academic profession. This change in style seemed as likely to have a devastating effect on Turkish institutions as the concomitant cutback in funds to maintain salaries and support services would.

4. *Sustained support over the economic cycle.* Abandon practices that make intellectual and professional support systems hostage to short-run financial exigencies. It must be appreciated that the continued sustenance of human capital through provision of adequate reference materials, libraries, and research assistance is as crucial to the survival of this capital as is the periodic maintenance and lubrication of physical capital. The required support systems will vary according to circumstances of the particular intellectuals and professionals but should include provision for regular interaction with the international community of peers through travel, attendance at meetings and seminars, hospitality to visitors, and research leaves abroad. A vigorous, creative

intellectual or professional life today is hardly possible in isolation from the global community; absence of contact is a recipe for obsolescence.

In discussing the multiple objectives pursued by many leaders and planners of higher education in developing countries, one Turkish scholar pleaded above all for clear recognition of the trade-off involved between quantity and quality. "When they give us huge classes to teach," he said, "they must realize it is at the expense of research. . . . If they destroy this generation of productive scholars in the process, they should know that they have eaten their seed corn and will have to pay the price down the road."

5. *Planned refreshment and renewal.* Provide for the systematic retraining and continuing education of high-level manpower in all fields. Both public and private authorities should be sensitized to this need and be creative in devising and sustaining the necessary institutional forms — be they classes, seminars, workshops, specialized conferences, or other devices. These authorities should resist the temptation to say "keeping up is the responsibility of the individual." Prevention of decay can best be effected collectively; since its benefits accrue to employer and employee alike, so should its costs. As a useful reminder of the prevention problem, employers might require highly skilled employees to address periodically the techniques they propose to employ to keep abreast of their disciplines or professions.

In the developed countries, as much as in the developing ones, certain areas of intellectual endeavor, most notably clinical medicine and business administration, have been more disposed to recognize the need for continuing education than others have. In some disciplines of the arts and sciences, in contrast, even to suggest the existence of such a need is to question the integrity and legitimacy of those in the field. In the developed countries, the problem may be less acute because continuing education occurs to some degree automatically through personal contacts, transmission of ideas by the sophisticated media, professional gatherings, and research. But prejudice and skeptical attitudes toward education beyond the terminal degree are clearly a barrier in both places.

Ironically, the need for periodic upgrading of skills is recognized worldwide for relatively low-level manpower — technicians, clerical employees, and so forth. Yet it is at the highest levels that both sensitivities and needs are greatest. To the extent that developing countries are able to exact conditions from multinational corporations wishing to operate within their borders, they may wish to specify that refreshment of other local personnel, in addition to their own personnel, will be required of them. This responsibility may be fulfilled by provision for technical courses, maintenance of a specialized library, cooperation with local institutions for adult education, and other devices.

6. *Nourishment and support of professional and intellectual communities.* Work self-consciously to build and sustain the aggregate community necessary to sustain high-level intellectuals and professionals. Manifestations of this community may include meetings, conferences, periodicals, and joint undertakings of various kinds. Aspects of this community should include networks and subnetworks of specialists on particular topics that will provide stim-

ulation, information, encouragement, criticism, standards, and a sense of self-worth. Institutions such as a national academy of science or an association for the advancement of science or the humanities, operated by scientists and humanists, should be developed to strengthen the intellectual community, to act as a public advocate for its needs, to publish periodicals, to sponsor applied research of national significance, to establish high aspirations, and to foster élan among members. Local awards of merit and prizes, preferably based on international peer review, can help to dramatize the values needed to sustain continued high-level efforts.

Repeatedly we heard reference to a sort of Rostovian stage theory of intellectual growth in Third World countries (discussed above). The most difficult task, the theory's advocates maintained, is to bring the intellectual community to a level of self-sustaining growth. To the extent that this argument has merit, stimulative institutions, like national academies, have a vital role to play, very much as their counterparts (e.g., The Royal Society of London) did at an earlier period in the West. They can establish scholarly values and targets for achievement. They can facilitate both the cooperative and competitive activities upon which intellectual life depends. They can provide a crucial window on the wider intellectual world. Public encouragement to intellectual life, through mechanisms such as this, clearly has a productive role to play, just as isolation, restriction, and exclusion of ideas are bound to have a counterproductive role.

Widespread recognition of the existence and importance of a scientific and intellectual community can of itself go some distance toward solving the problem of decay. When concern is manifest, employees will be encouraged and assisted in their efforts to keep up, not from altruism on the part of their employers but from self-interest. Private firms competing on an open world market, in fact, have no alternatives to acquisition of the best skills and technology and pursuit of research and development. It is likely that in the public sector, where the absence of market penalties prevails, obsolescence of human and physical capital will proceed unimpeded.

7. *Involvement in national development.* Whenever possible, provide intellectuals and professionals with opportunities to respond creatively to national needs. These people must not be perceived by themselves, or by others, to be inhabiting a remote compound and performing functions of interest mainly to themselves. It is usually possible, though sometimes difficult, to discover challenging questions of both local and broad intellectual interest in any discipline or profession. Efforts to address these challenges can be sustained by government through programs of support for very broadly conceived relevant research and consultancies. One Turkish economist reported, with evident regret, that he consulted extensively for international organizations but was never asked for advice by his own government. He expressed the hope that he could shift the balance more to "become a part of Turkey" than to stay a part of the international community.

The results of a program of government support for relevant research can include answers to important questions, sustenance of an embryonic community of inquirers, and the ultimate strengthening of ties between those respon-

66

sible for forming and implementing policy and those able to cast valuable light on it. One Turkish academic who had recently, and grudgingly, taken a part-time position in industry to supplement his meager professorial salary told us with some surprise that this experience of becoming visibly productive at his craft had been unexpectedly stimulating. This led him to urge more general exploration of opportunities for closer links between intellectuals and professionals and the burgeoning private sector, as well as the government.

The practice of placing students as interns in either the public sector or industry did not seem to be part of the culture of any of the three countries we visited. We suggest that internships can be a way of laying the foundation for mutually beneficial academic-industrial relationships in later life.

Extension services by schools of agriculture have always been seen by us as an exceptionally desirable form of interaction between the academic and the practical. Therefore, we regretted that the provision of such services by universities had recently been prohibited in one of the countries we visited.

8. The open academy. So as to further cement the ties between the intellectual and political communities, and thereby to strengthen and extend the network of relationships between "thinkers" and "doers," encourage the participation of qualified public officials in research and teaching programs of universities and research laboratories. Although hazards to the maintenance of high scholarly standards do exist in such a partnership, the benefits in terms of improved understanding and stimulation on both sides are worth the effort. It is important for academia to maintain a welcoming, respectful attitude toward the participation of practitioners in teaching and research, but the ultimate leadership and authority in these arenas must naturally remain with the professional scholars.

9. The magnet universities. Make arrangements for the most distinguished local educational institutions to take the leadership in the effort to resist intellectual and professional decay throughout society. Continuing education, even for manpower at the highest levels, tends now to have low priority at the most prestigious institutions throughout the world; it is often a task thrust upon them. If this attitude can be changed, however, these institutions may find the task, although demanding, exceptionally rewarding. They will discover that these efforts to help others remain in the vanguard are valuable to their own faculty and staff, in addition to those they regularly serve. Each institution may wish to take responsibility for the intellectual and professional health of one region of the country, or of several subject areas, cooperating with other, more privileged institutions in providing a network of support.

Accompanying a commitment from the elite teaching and research institutions of a nation to accept responsibility for the intellectual health of their community must be a commitment from the nation to sustain these institutions in their privileged positions. In all three of the countries we visited, we heard anguished cries from academic leaders about attempts to cut down the "tall poppies" of higher education; the stronger universities felt severely threatened by injunctions to serve a vastly increased undergraduate student body at the expense of graduate teaching and research. Productive research scholars and graduate faculty complained of a leveling policy that distributed resources and teaching loads evenly throughout higher education.

One of the most effective arguments that can be employed against this trend is the need to sustain the unique role of research universities, not only for their distinctive products but also for the health and welfare of the faculty members in the institutions where the bulk of the undergraduate teaching is performed. If existing elite universities are unwilling to play the role of "magnet" institutions, serving in part the intellectual and professional communities throughout the nation, it may be desirable to create new universities specifically to address this need. The Australian National University in Canberra is one attractive model. It was created by another "new" country after World War II to retain and attract back to its shores the country's most distinguished native sons and to serve the wider intellectual community of Australia.

10. Pursuit of scholarly comparative advantage. Seek to identify and exploit areas of research that are of potential domestic significance but that are also manageable with local resources and grow out of the comparative advantage of the local research community. To have some research programs that are truly world class, despite a paucity of equipment and support services, seems to have a positive psychological effect on research scholars that transcends the actual value of the research product. We encountered several examples of these programs, including one in Mexico on the medicinal properties of desert plants; another on large-scale networking of microcomputers; another on laboratory equipment suitable for developing countries; and one in Turkey on Middle East economic history.

In the social sciences we found excitement generated in all three countries by the study of "re-democratization," a subject of immense local interest on which Third World political scientists understandably have become the leading authorities. This subject area calls out for comparative analysis in all relevant developing countries; scholars in these countries can expect to encounter a rapt audience throughout the world. Women's studies is another area in which we found great interest and substantial accomplishment in all three developing countries.

The obverse of the injunction to pursue research and teaching that conform to local comparative advantage is to refrain from pursuing subjects for which the local demand is slight and the required resources are inadequate. This suggests little attention to, for example, particle physics or aeronautical engineering.

A frequent complaint we heard about most refreshment activities was the extent to which they are a one-way street, from north to south as it were. The development of selected world-class areas of endeavor will help to render this flow two-way.

We were warned that there is a dangerous tendency in new nations to take the "easy way out" and encourage loose armchair theorizing in certain research areas. Several persons claimed that in most cases what would make research in the Third World truly unique and internationally valuable is the painstaking pursuit of empirical studies using the wealth of data available to them.

11. The market for renewal. Encourage, or at least do not discourage, the growth of commercial "intellectual aftercare providers" — domestic or multinational profit-making firms or nonprofit institutions of various kinds that develop and market decay-prevention services on a self-sustaining basis. Nations that encourage these enterprises have very little to lose and much to gain. Some countries have already permitted these enterprises to grow up in such fields as business education, accounting, and clinical medicine, and there seems to be no reason why the principle cannot be extended much more widely.

There seems to be no limit to the innovative devices that can come from these providers; devices include advanced refresher courses, review journals, and specialized seminars on the "state of the art" in particular areas. We were told by some firms that first-class aftercare services had become more important to many senior employees than salary increases. There is undoubtedly some danger of unscrupulous charlatanism in the provision of aftercare, as in all higher education, but we suspect that with the mature adults who constitute this market the familiar advice "caveat emptor" is more effective protection than any kind of regulation.

We talked with staff of one large multinational bank who viewed the provision of aftercare services to potential clients as a promising way to explore new markets. This seemed to be a practice from which everyone gained. Several Turkish businessmen who had purchased the services of commercial aftercare providers said they preferred those with international client groups, including Americans. They said the seriousness of these programs reminded them of their graduate-student days in the United States.

12. English, the lingua franca. Take steps to maintain the facility of professionals and intellectuals in both written and spoken English. Like it or not, English has become the lingua franca for scholarly and professional communication, and those who lose their competence in its use are quickly cut off from advances in their fields. Loss of oral facility destroys the capacity to benefit fully from participation in international meetings and association with foreign visitors. Loss of ease in reading cuts off or reduces contact with advances in a discipline. Discomfort in writing English prevents a scholar from making contributions to those parts of the scholarly literature that will have widest impact and will bring honored membership in the leadership of the international community.

Preservation of English facility among an intellectual community in which English is a second language requires imagination, creativity, persistence, and commitment. In our travels, we discovered few programs that had this end specifically in mind, although study leaves and periodic foreign travel were partly addressed to this end. Easy access to language classes and other linguistic facilities for initial training and later retooling is highly desirable, as are regular local scholarly and professional gatherings conducted in English.

In Turkey, we visited one language training school where some students and instructors said their participation in conversation classes was aimed as much at retention of old skill levels as at acquisition of new ones. They also testified to the value of watching English-language television and listening to

English radio programs (in this case, broadcasts from Greece) for the sustenance of their skills. It seemed regrettable that the education in English being delivered to U.S. citizens (mainly military personnel under the auspices of the U.S. Federal Government) in the countries we visited could not be shared with local citizens who wished to sustain their language facility. In this regard, we heard high praise for USIS-published periodicals for teachers of English.

13. Graduate education: seedbed and transmission belt. Recognize the important function of graduate education as a device for sustaining and replenishing human capital, as well as for creating it in the first place. We encountered numerous examples of young postgraduate training programs that played a central role in retarding decay, both by offering refresher courses to the staff of their own and neighboring institutions and by sending their own senior predoctoral students abroad for brief periods (normally one year) to learn about and on their return report on what was happening on the frontier of their subjects in other countries. If constructed wisely and used effectively, postgraduate education can become an effective transmission belt for ideas, techniques, and the identification of topical priorities. It can also be one of the simplest devices for sustaining standards at international levels.

14. The value of doctorate completion. Make every effort to see that those students who go abroad for doctoral study do complete the full program, especially the thesis or dissertation. We encountered wide differences in cultural attitudes toward failure to complete a degree program. In some places, as in the United States, failure to finish terminated an academic or professional career. In others, the mere fact of having "studied abroad" seemed enough to guarantee status and prestige, and degree completion seemed almost irrelevant. All the same, we sensed that those people who had not completed the full degree requirements and thus remained the proverbial A.B.D.'s (all but dissertations) were far less likely than those who did complete to enter the global marketplace of ideas confidently and with something to give as well as to take. If nothing else, completion of the thesis or dissertation provides a young scholar with one potentially publishable research product and an open ticket to international scholarly recognition, at least for several years. Failure to complete, on the other hand, is likely to be one more blow to scholarly self-confidence and morale, which may not have been very strong in the first place.

We recommend a combination of carrots and sticks to ensure degree completion. Institutions in the less developed countries, like those in the developed countries, should impose serious sanctions, such as loss of appointment, against those who do not complete. By and large, we sense a far too relaxed attitude on this point. These institutions should not only be more strict but also make every effort to facilitate completion through provision of facilities and released time, and they should reward junior scholars for publication in the international community of their discipline. A mind that is active and engaged, optimistic and excited, and even slightly intoxicated by the smell of printer's ink, is less likely to decay and draw down its neighbors. The practice in one country we visited of rewarding completion of the degree by induction into military service seemed especially unwise. Not only was the incentive perverse, but premature decay was also virtually assured.

Policies and Practices for the Developed World

1. Specialized renewal mechanisms. Create and nurture programs and institutions in the developed world that are designed to assist the developing countries with their problems of intellectual and professional decay. It is possible, in principle, for a developed nation to set up at home a project concerned exclusively with the aftercare of intellectual and professional personnel from the developing world. However, in practice, it appears to be more sensible and profitable for this purpose to attach a component to programs or institutions with a wider function, including aftercare on the home front and, more generally, teaching and research.

A number of U.S. institutions do in fact play this dual role of pursuing other larger goals while helping to sustain the vigor of the professional and intellectual communities of the developing world. Examples are the United States/Mexico Program at the University of California at San Diego; the Woodrow Wilson International Center for Scholars and the Institute for International Economics (both in Washington, D.C.); and the Center for International Affairs at Harvard University. The program opportunities are virtually limitless for extending the focus of these and comparable institutions to provide regularly for visiting participants from the developing world whose objective is refreshment. Resources are the principal constraint.

Practically all those with whom we talked stressed the value of sustained institution-to-institution relationships that lead to continuous, cumulative linkages rather than simply to ad hoc contacts. One individual even referred to the need for "postdoctoral mentors." In a few cases, "twinning" of institutions in the United States and in developing countries has worked very well.

2. Refreshment visits. Construct and sustain fellowship programs for visitors from the developing world to spend varying amounts of time in activities that help restore their skills, contacts, and competencies. Two conspicuously successful programs, the American Studies Program of the American Council of Learned Societies and the Fulbright Program for visiting foreign scholars, are described earlier in this report. These programs and others like them should be recognized, respected, supported, and cherished for the exceptionally valuable aftercare functions they perform.

Somewhat to our surprise, we encountered among our contacts great enthusiasm for fellowship programs that have a "practical" or "in-service" component. Among all the advanced professional disciplines, and among scientists and social scientists as well, there was high praise for periods of time spent in firms; public authorities; federal, state and local governments; professional firms of doctors, lawyers, architects, and engineers; hospitals; and virtually every other area of American professional life. Some excellent arrangements already exist for such placement, including the Hubert Humphrey North-South Fellowship Program, but it appears that others are needed.

It was put to us that refreshment in many of the most valuable aspects of American intellectual and professional style can be gained most effectively in a work environment. The following features were listed as qualities to be renewed in this way: flexibility, outspokenness, capacity to pace oneself, emphasis on creativity, effectiveness in one-to-one contact, and informality across the hierarchy. A Turkish architect told us how he had arranged his own period of exchange and refreshment with a U.S. firm by answering advertisements in American newspapers. He was ecstatic about the result. He believed that everyone had gained from the arrangement. He had been young, vigorous, and inexpensive for the American employer (helping to design Disney World and the Grand Ole Opry!), and he remained their close contact in Turkey. For himself, he had gained a practical education that he could have never gained in any faculty of architecture.

We were equally surprised to hear repeated pleas in all three countries for U.S. fellowship programs to be kept firmly under the control of American managers. Our interviewees worried that local government participation would allow wide swings in disciplinary priority according to current fashion and might even introduce criteria for selection other than merit determined by peer review.

3. Refreshment visitors. Enable visitors from the developed countries to make contributions of various kinds to the refreshment of professionals and intellectuals in the developing countries. However, the visits must be planned carefully and their purposes thoroughly understood.

It is possible to categorize the types of visits. First, distinguished leaders of fields can be brought in for short periods (several days to several weeks) to talk, stimulate, develop contacts, and advise on research and curriculum. Our experience indicates that these visits can work well, or very badly, depending on circumstances. Above all, distinguished visitors with the right sympathies must be recruited, and their visits must be scheduled to make the very best use of their time. Ideally they should spend most of their energies on the equivalent of "master classes" in the arts, working with highly talented younger scholars and scientists to provide the meaningful guidance and encouragement that is lacking in the local community. Such visits may initiate continuing contacts and even joint research projects. It is worth stressing, however, that such visitors can have far greater impact working with the faculty of their host institution than concentrating on teaching classes to large numbers of students.

Second, junior scholars in the First World, typically those who have just completed advanced degrees, can be brought for visits. These scholars can be expected to bring an understanding of both recent and long-term developments in fields to their new colleagues. These younger scholars can also be expected to accept substantial teaching loads at both graduate and undergraduate levels. If the visits are sponsored by an assistance agency, a condition of them should be that the "released time" made available in Third World institutions is used to support the research of indigenous faculty, not simply to relieve some institutional budget. A long-term benefit for junior visitors is that they can develop lifelong interest in and commitment to the host countries, facilitating repeat visits and joint projects when they return home.

Third, visits that seem to be growing in popularity are return visits, for varying periods, by expatriate natives of Third World countries who have settled abroad permanently and have made distinguished international reputations. These persons, perhaps motivated by a mixture of affection, responsibility, and guilt, are often ready to make major sacrifices to respond to the decay problems of their countrymen. They also can appreciate the particular complexities of the local challenges and accomplish far more in a given time than someone coming in entirely cold.

Finally, fourth, visits that we discern to be of least value to the recipient country are those by undistinguished older scholars and professionals from the First World who are themselves experiencing serious decay and losing touch with their fields. Our impression is that, under some exchange programs, this type of visit has increased and that contributions by such visits are, in extreme cases, of a negative sort. The image of an American scholar or professional who can no longer master a field's literature, engage in significant research, or publish on the frontier can be profoundly discouraging to a person in a new country who is attempting to do all these things while dealing with the substantial difficulties of the local environment. "If he can't do it with all his advantages, how can I?" may be the reaction. One senior administrator at a Turkish university said she no longer permitted visits from participants in one prominent American exchange program because they were of this type. Even though foreign experience may be of personal benefit to almost any American scholar, we think more attention should be paid to the limited benefits the scholar can confer on those he or she visits.

A particular device for assisting with midcareer refreshment in the Third World, developed by the military, caught our attention. Aid to friendly armed forces is provided by the United States with the advice of resident experts, called Military Assistance Groups (MAGs). (See the separate discussion in the section on Turkish cases.) One of the devices employed by the MAGs is the mobile training team (MTT), which consists of several American experts who are sent around a country on a whirlwind tour, refreshing the indigenous military on topics as diverse as tactics and welding. Two decades of experience have shown this device to work well for the armed forces. We think it may work as well for civilian retraining.

A small team of highly skilled and personally distinguished American specialists might, we believe, make substantial contributions to the direction, morale, range of contacts, objectives, and technical competence of scholars and scientists in the countries we visited. Moreover, the scope of the MTT tours, from four to six weeks overall, is within the practical range of persons with the distinction appropriate for the task. One variant of the MTT notion might be to substitute longer stops for the series of shorter ones. A model for this variant is the Kyoto Seminar on American Studies, operated annually and very successfully in Japan for more than 20 years.

4. Cooperative research. Engage in truly cooperative, balanced research and scholarly endeavors with intellectuals and professionals from the developing world. Cooperative research has been undertaken in recent years, supported by, for example, the National Science Foundation, as described earlier. However, much more is possible and desirable. Projects of this genre provide a range of opportunities for a positive-sum game among the countries involved and should be encouraged self-consciously by individuals and agencies responsible for the humanities and the professions, as well as for the hard sciences, where the tradition of cooperative team research is better established.

Many leaders in the developing world emphasize the high potential payoff they perceive in this strategy, but they insist on the desirability of developing-country initiative whenever possible and, at least, on a balance among the partners in planning and execution ("not just working for the gringo"). It was suggested that the most promising areas of inquiry were quite basic in form but potentially applicable to problems of the developing countries, for example, questions related to photosynthesis, strength of materials, and tax incentives.

5. Creative institutional responses. In the widest sense, apply well-known American ingenuity to producing innovative devices to assist the developing world in resisting professional and intellectual decay.

Suggestions that we heard during our travels included new devices for scholarly communication, such as reviews and digests of scholarly literature, newsletters, bibliographies, and, above all, low-cost periodicals for export to the developing world. We were asked repeatedly whether it might not be possible for Western publishers of periodicals to engage in systematic price discrimination in favor of the developing world (perhaps sales at marginal cost) or at least to provide for the free deposit of small numbers of their products at a set of central repositories in the Third World. One young Turkish faculty member appealed for a periodical publication in her field that would tell her, in all candor and after careful reflection, just which books she simply must buy for her personal library. She noted that in her case the average price of a U.S. book was equal to one week's salary.

In addition to publications, American universities and professional associations should experiment with short (one-month) crash courses on relatively narrow subjects to bring up to speed scholars and professionals who have long since completed higher education and, while still active, are faced with inhibiting obsolescence. We were told of very successful examples of such courses given by the Survey Research Center at the University of Michigan on sampling techniques and the Arthur Andersen accounting firm on advanced accounting practices. Short courses are both less expensive to run than long ones and far easier for senior scholars and professionals to attend.

While the search should continue for new support mechanisms, old ones should not be neglected. The USIA libraries abroad, for example, are particular resources that are becoming crucial to intellectual survival in all three countries.

6. American university responsibilities. Accept specific aftercare responsibilities for alumni in developing countries. Fulfillment of this responsibility by American universities can include creation of a regular set of visiting return fellowships to the home campus, dispatch of faculty for lecture tours abroad, and, in general, assistance with the wide range of problems that arise with the acquisition of publications. In fact, numerous individual faculty members at various American universities have informally assumed this role, especially those who have themselves served abroad on assistance projects. This admirable volunteerism is, however, no adequate substitute for a systematic effort. It should no longer be the case that a Third World scholar hears from his alma mater only when there is an appeal for funds.

7. Long-term development linkages. Look beyond the termination of training programs. All assistance projects with an educational component in which American donors take part, through private agencies like foundations and church groups, bilateral public assistance agencies like AID, or multilateral agencies like the World Bank, should pay specific attention to the aftercare implications of projects. If the intent is to build up human capital, they should demonstrate how this capital is to be serviced and maintained. If necessary, they should make provision in the initial contract for reasonable maintenance over a limited period of time.

Above all, assistance agencies must be sensitized to the seriousness of intellectual and professional obsolescence and to its extended time horizon so that they will be prepared to respond to them when the occasions arise. We suggest that the traditional view that educational assistance comes to an abrupt halt with the termination of formal programs is naive, even wasteful. All educational assistance projects should have an extended afterlife so that resources are available to maintain the human capital that is constructed. In cases in which the original assistance project is based on close linkages between American and developing-country institutions (e.g., universities, planning departments, and research laboratories), provisions should be made to sustain the links.

In cases in which accelerated deterioration has occurred during the crises of recent years, we urge assistance agencies to consider selected emergency rescue operations involving such actions as one-time catch-up library grants and refreshment fellowships for exceptional persons whose decline is not too severe.

8. The global audience. In a general sense, self-consciously endeavor to provide an audience for specialized intellectuals in the developing countries who otherwise may languish in isolation. After a while it seems futile to speak if there are few listeners in the countries of the world, so attentive ears can be powerful incentives. The issue is not whether or not the skills of the isolated intellectuals are truly valuable to their homeland. Even the bearers of exceptionally valuable but highly specialized skills may feel lonely, frustrated, and without challenge because they are distant from a community of their own kind. A small new nation may desperately need one or two top-notch hydrologists, but probably not more. Can these one or two be helped to have a satisfying and productive career in isolation? To help make this possible, without drawing permanently to its own shores the intellectual and professional resources it wishes to serve abroad, is the challenge that the developed world has yet to face.

IIE RESEARCH SERIES

Report #1
ABSENCE OF DECISION:
(not available)
Foreign Students in American Colleges and Universities

Craufurd D. Goodwin
Michael Nacht

Report #2
BLACK EDUCATION IN SOUTH AFRICA:
The Current Situation

David R. Smock

Report #3
A SURVEY OF POLICY CHANGES:
Foreign Students in Public Institutions of Higher Education

Elinor G. Barber

Report #4
THE ITT INTERNATIONAL FELLOWSHIP PROGRAM:
An Assessment After Ten Years

Marianthi Zikopoulos
Elinor G. Barber

Report #5
FONDNESS AND FRUSTRATION:
The Impact of American Higher Education on Foreign Students with Special
Reference to the Case of Brazil

Craufurd D. Goodwin
Michael Nacht

Report #6
INTERNATIONAL EXPERTISE IN AMERICAN BUSINESS:
How to Learn to Play with the Kids on the Street

Stephen J. Kobrin

Report #7
FOREIGN STUDENT FLOWS:
Their Significance for American Higher Education

Elinor G. Barber

Report #8
A SURVEY OF POLICY CHANGES:
Foreign Students in Public Institutions of Higher Education from 1983 to 1985

William J. McCann, Jr.

For further information on publications listed here, please contact:
Elinor Barber
Manager, Research Department
Institute of International Education
809 United Nations Plaza
New York, NY 10017
212-984-5346